LIBERTY AGAINST
GOVERNMENT

LIBERTY AGAINST

GOVERNMENT

*The Rise, Flowering
and Decline of a Famous
Juridical Concept*

By

EDWARD S. CORWIN

1948
LOUISIANA STATE UNIVERSITY PRESS
Baton Rouge

TO

C. W. T.

GRACIOUS HOSTESS, STANCH
FRIEND—TO HER HOST OF FRIENDS
A HOST IN HERSELF

❧ FOREWORD

T HE HISTORY of American liberty is far more complicated than most people would at first blush have imagined. Indeed, until Professor Corwin, out of a lifetime of
study devoted to American public law, distilled into a volume of modest compass the essential ingredients of American liberty, there was, to my knowledge, no one book to
which the citizen might turn to learn its fascinating story.
The story starts, as do so many of the great things of life,
with the Greeks and the Romans. The wisdom of the political philosophers, ancient and modern, in their search for
the foundations of human liberty is presented in its relation
to the crucial events of English and American political
experience, particularly such great documents as Magna
Carta, the Declaration of Independence, the federal Constitution and our State constitutions. The impact of political doctrine and written constitutions on individual
controversies involving fundamental rights is traced in the
leading decisions of our highest courts. But where the political theory of bygone ages ordinarily is nebulous and
unreal, and court decisions on constitutional issues inter-
minably long and often inexcusably involved, here Professor Corwin has employed his rare gift of condensation
to state in single paragraphs the gist of abstract doctrines,

of controlling political and economic situations, and of judicial controversies which have elsewhere taken entire chapters and even volumes. We are thus enabled not only to see the successive problems of our constitutional development but to envision them in their relation to each other. We sense the intellectual and emotional struggles of the judges in their efforts to decide fundamental issues affecting the life of the entire nation. Professor Corwin, withal, has contrived to keep his presentation of the involved problems of liberty as a juridical concept almost delusively simple without being a mere tour de force.

Property has been frequently described as a bundle of rights. Even more is liberty a bundle of rights, rights which have been buttressed from time to time by a wide variety of political doctrines and constitutional provisions. The study of the history of American liberty is complicated by the fact that here more than in any other branch of the law have words had a way of changing their meaning to fit new situations. Sometimes, however, old words and old doctrines fade away and new words, like reinforcements, come forward to take their place. Professor Corwin does not fail to keep us advised of such transitions. Not only do words and doctrines change but social attitudes; a Constitution designed for an age of individualism quite free from governmental restraints has been made to serve the needs of an interdependent society more accustomed to governmental regulation.

Professor Corwin guides us skillfully through the labyrinth of the decisions of the United States Supreme Court on liberty under the federal Constitution. We come to realize by the end of our journey that the course of decisions was by no means an inevitable one. Time and place and personalities all played their part. Though the course was not inevitable, it has gone far to dictate to us what the future will be. The extent to which we may still control it depends largely upon our knowledge, on the one hand, of the actualities of American life today and, on the other hand, on our comprehension of the development of our constitutional concept of liberty as Professor Corwin has analyzed it. Especially noteworthy is the extent to which our liberty has been controlled by matters of procedure, the doctrine of judicial notice among others.

"A word," says Mr. Justice Holmes, "is not a crystal, transparent and unchanging, it is the skin of a living thought and may vary greatly in color and content according to the circumstances and time in which it is used." How true this is of "liberty" as a concept Professor Corwin's scholarly work clearly demonstrates. He brings home to us a very real sense of the difficulties of maintaining liberty under law. No longer will we be tempted to think of it as a simple process, much less as our birthright, ours for the asking. The history of liberty as a juristic concept may well cause us to ponder as to its future.

ARTHUR T. VANDERBILT, CHIEF JUSTICE
NEW JERSEY SUPREME COURT

PREFACE

Nearly fifty years ago I had the good fortune to take with Professor Andrew C. McLaughlin (better known in those days as "Andy Mac") his celebrated course in American Constitutional History. I was then a senior at the University of Michigan. When we came to study the Dred Scott case, I drew Professor McLaughlin's attention to that sentence in Chief Justice Taney's opinion in which section 8 of the Missouri Compromise was stigmatized as *not* "due process of law." Since no judicial proceedings appeared to be involved in the case, this statement puzzled me. "What," I asked Professor McLaughlin, "does he mean there by 'due process of law'?" Obviously embarrassed, Professor McLaughlin replied, "I don't know." Well, I felt, if he doesn't know, nobody does; and it occurred to me that the subject might possibly be worth looking into sometime.

As it happened, the search was considerably delayed, but in an article which I published in the *Michigan Law Review* in June, 1909, the first fruits of it appear. I there pointed out that "due process of law" originally meant due process for the *enforcement* of the law, but that in such cases as Lochner v. New York—then a recent story —the term had come to mean a "reasonable" exercise of the police power—i.e., such exercise of the police power as the Supreme Court held to be *reasonable;* and I speculated briefly as to how the latter conception of "due process of law" could have been derived from the former. But that, obviously, was only to *state* the problem; although, as I felt, a step too toward solving it, since, as Professor Dicey points out, it is sometimes actually more difficult to make people see that there *is* a problem than to make them, once they have seen it, comprehend its solution.

The solution itself, or what I believed to be such, was developed in my articles on "The Doctrine of Due Process of Law before the Civil War," which appeared in the *Harvard Law Review* for April and May, 1911, and in one on "The Basic Doctrine of American Constitutional Law," which came out in the *Michigan Law Review* for February, 1914. Then—to make a long story short—fourteen years later I brought out in the *Harvard Law Review* for December, 1928, and January, 1929, two articles entitled "The 'Higher Law' Background of American Constitutional Law," in which I traced the doctrine of "reasonableness" to its Roman and English sources. In 1938 the last five of the articles just listed were republished in their original form in *Selected Essays on Constitutional Law.*

The immediate occasion for the preparation of the present volume was an invitation by the Louisiana State University Press to expand into a book a lecture which I gave at that institution in May, 1943, under the auspices of the Edward Douglass White Foundation. The substance of the lecture itself is incorporated in Chapters I and V of the present volume. The invitation was accepted with gratitude, as it gave me the opportunity to do what I had long planned to do, namely, present as a continuous story the oldest theme which underlies the history of American constitutional law, that of *Liberty Against Government*. This design has of course compelled extensive rewriting and revision of the studies listed previously. The argument has been reshaped, much matter has been discarded, much new matter has been added. For this work, I have drawn on an even dozen previously published studies of mine and two unpublished ones, and I have benefited by the perspective afforded by recent developments.

Indeed, I feel that this small volume, while by no means designed to be a tract for the times, is nevertheless a very timely one. But perhaps I had better leave that, as well as the rest of its virtues, for others to judge.

To the acknowledgments already made I wish to add a few more personal ones. I am greatly indebted to my former student and good friend Professor Robert J. Harris, Jr., for his helpful interest in the publication of this volume; to Marcus M. Wilkerson, Director of the Louisiana State University Press, for his unfailing diligence, patience, and encouragement; to Mary Lamury Smith of the Press staff for her most intelligent editing of the manuscript; and to Alma Fell for her swift and accurate work in typing. Finally, I wish to thank my friend Professor Charles H. McIlwain for reading part of the work in page proof, and Chief Justice Arthur T. Vanderbilt for his great kindness in preparing the Foreword.

EDWARD S. CORWIN

CONTENTS

"IT IS TO SECURE OUR RIGHTS THAT WE
RESORT TO GOVERNMENT AT ALL."

THOMAS JEFFERSON (*1795*)

CHAPTER I

LIBERTY AS A JURIDICAL CONCEPT

THE CENTRAL theme of this volume is the rise, development, and decline of that distinctively American employment of the word "liberty," which treats it as a constitutional limitation, enforcible by courts upon the legislative branch of government—*liberty*, in brief, as a *juridical concept*. The story reaches back of the beginning of the Christian Era and comes down through the most recent term of the United States Supreme Court. It is also a fairly continuous story and a nearly complete one. Whether, indeed, it *is* a complete—a *completed*—story is itself an interesting question, one which I shall leave with the reader.

But before entering upon our historical inquiry it will be of advantage to disentangle "liberty" as a title of American constitutional law from certain other connotations of the word. We shall not be interested, in these pages, in "liberty" as a shibboleth of politicians, a theme of hymn makers, an inspiration of poetic raptures. Sweeping over-all definitions of the word may be considered as discarded from the outset. I have one of that kind before me as I write—a definition of "freedom" (it might as well be "liberty") as "ability to do what you want." [1] The definition is pert, but obviously not pertinent to the ever challenging problem of how to reconcile one man's liberty with another's.

Nor are we obliged to give attention to that species of "liberty" the source of which is personal capacity, the wealth and variety of the individual's own endowment of character, ability, versatility, even at times lack of moral scruples. Thus the late Führer was accustomed to boast of his "hardness," and his acts did not belie him in this respect. Nor was Hitler's ideal, Napoleon, appreciably hindered by a conscience. Likewise, we may pass by all purely subjective conceptions of liberty—like *Kraft durch Freude*, the freedom of the Great Open Spaces, the freedom of immersion in the Life of the City, and the kind of freedom which, according to the authoritative exponent of Soviet Philosophy, is enjoyed in the U.S.S.R., "freedom from the individual's responsibility of reaching critical conclusions about anything on which the State, i.e. the Communist Party, has taken a position." [2]

Lastly, we may discard as irrelevant the conception of liberty which is urged by the so-called Idealist School of Political Thought, and which, on one ground or another, merges the individual with society and on this premise stipulates for the former only that liberty which contributes to social well-being as this is authoritatively determined by society. It must be acknowledged that the

[1] Barbara Wootton, *Freedom Under Planning* (University of North Carolina, 1945), 6, 15.

[2] Sidney Hook, reviewing John Somerville's *Soviet Philosophy; A Study of Theory and Practice*, in *The Nation*, February 15, 1947.

individual is always dependent on membership in a community, and in a *politically organized community*, for even a minimum of liberty; but this concession affords no assurance that the community will always be willing to guarantee or prepared to maintain the individual— even "the man of good will"—in the full measure of liberty which he expects, and which many of his fellows think he has a right to expect.

And whatever the origin of liberty, whether it should be deemed to precede the establishment of government or not, once government is established there are bound to arise from time to time conditions of tension between it and some of the human beings who are amenable to its powers. Such conditions of tension are, in fact, of the first importance in instigating efforts at social change. Yet such efforts, however fully they may meet the expectations of their authors, rarely satisfy all persons who are affected by them, and those who remain dissatisfied may be counted on to protest in the name of "liberty," "justice," and the like, and are entitled to do so under a regime of political freedom.

Liberty, in the sense here used, always implies the distinct and independent identity of the individual from the political order of which he is a member. It also implies the right of the individual to make certain claims upon the political order. Basically such claims are of two types: first, *the claim that government protect the claimant in the safe continuance of his existing way of life;* second, *the claim that government contribute something to the improvement of the claimant's way of life.*

The latter, the reformist type of claim, was strikingly voiced by the late President Roosevelt in his surprise message to Congress of January 11, 1944. In this message Mr. Roosevelt sought to sugar-coat a demand that Congress authorize a conscription of labor for the remainder of the war with a recitation of certain demands which, he argued, citizens of the United States were today entitled to make of government.

The program which the message sketched was breath-taking in scope, but boiled down to a guarantee of "economic security and independence," which the President contended to be essential if even the older types of "freedom" were to retain practical significance for the common man. " 'Necessitous men,' " he quoted, " 'are not free men.' " [3]

[3] The salient passages of the message were as follows:

"This Republic had its beginning, and grew to its present strength, under the protection of certain inalienable political rights—among them the right of free speech, free press, free worship, trial by jury, freedom from unreasonable searches and seizures. They were our rights to life and liberty.

"As our nation has grown in size and stature, however—as our industrial economy expanded—these political rights proved inadequate to assure us equality in the pursuit of happiness.

"We have come to a clear realization of the fact that true individual freedom cannot exist without economic security and independence. 'Necessitous men are not free men.' People who are hungry and out of a job are the stuff of which dictatorships are made.

"In our day these economic truths have become accepted as self-evident. We have accepted, so to speak, a second Bill of Rights under which a new basis of security and prosperity can be established for all, regardless of station, race or creed.

"Among these are:

"The right to a useful and remunerative job in the industries or shops or farms or mines of the nation;

"The right to earn enough to provide adequate food and clothing and recreation;

"The right of every farmer to raise and sell his products at a return which will give him and his family a decent living;

Nor, indeed, is this reformist conception of liberty, for which its exponents nowadays appear to prefer the term "freedom," something without precedent from our own past. In three important respects at least did it contribute to the development and enrichment of American legislative policy of earlier times: in the establishment of public education, in the abolition of slavery, and in the extension of the suffrage. Each of these great reforms represented a positive gift from government which was intended to improve the lot in life and increase the personal significance of its beneficiaries; and the third is the foundation of American *political liberty*, the right of the people to choose their governors and to retire them at frequent intervals.

"The right of every business man, large and small, to trade in an atmosphere of freedom from unfair competition and domination by monopolies at home or abroad;

"The right of every family to a decent home;

"The right to adequate medical care and the opportunity to achieve and enjoy good health;

"The right to adequate protection from the economic fears of old age, sickness, accident and unemployment;

"The right to a good education.

"All these rights spell security. And after this war is won we must be prepared to move forward, in the implementation of these rights, to new goals of human happiness and well-being.

"America's own rightful place in the world depends in large part upon how fully these and similar rights have been carried into practice for our citizens. For unless there is security here at home there cannot be lasting peace in the world."

This declaration was repeated by Mr. Roosevelt in his Chicago speech of October 28, 1944. A report of the American Law Institute published in the New York *Times* of February 12, 1945, lists eight more "freedoms," or eighteen in all. The apothegm about "necessitous men" comes from the Lord Chancellor's opinion in Vernon *v.* Bethell, 2 Eden 113 (1762), whence it is extracted by Justice Curtis in his opinion in Russell *v.* Southard *et al.*, 12 How. 139 (1851).

But while the *reformist* conception of liberty and the *juridical* conception have a common rootage in the inevitable tensions of community life, they are otherwise antagonistic. The conflict between them is well illustrated in some remarks of President Lincoln, in 1864, apropos of the slavery issue. Said Mr. Lincoln: "The world has never had a good definition of the word liberty, and the American people, just now are much in want of one. We all declare for liberty; but in using the same *word* we do not all mean the same *thing*. With some the word liberty may mean for each man to do as he pleases with himself, and the product of his labor; while with others the same word may mean for some men to do as they please with other men, and the product of other men's labor. Here are two, not only different, but incompatible things, called by the same name, liberty. And it follows that each of the things is, by the respective parties, called by two different and incompatible names—liberty and tyranny." [4]

The incompatibility was, of course, authoritatively resolved in favor of the *reformist* conception of liberty when, in December 1865, the Thirteenth Amendment was added to the Constitution. Yet not everybody so accepted it at first, and in the *Democratic Almanac* of 1866, the Thirteenth Amendment was still vigorously assailed as "unconstitutional" because of its invasion of "vested rights."

In short, the conception of liberty with which liberty as a juridical concept is cognate is essentially *conservative* and *static*. What it demands of government is protection in the *continuance* of an existing mode of life and in the secure possession of the interests which sustain that mode

[4] *Writings* (Constitutional ed., 1906), VII, 121.

of life. But this does not mean, on the other hand, protection against unfavorable conditions as such, although these frequently furnish the reformer with the very substance of his grievance. The conditions against which the conservative demands protection comprise only those conditions in the causation of which there is, to the conservative's way of thinking at any rate, a traceable human complicity.

For the purposes of this study, therefore, *liberty signifies the absence of restraints imposed by other persons upon our own freedom of choice and action*—that, and nothing more recondite. But once again the subject dichotomizes itself, namely, along the line which separates *private* persons, our neighbors, as possible sources of restraints upon our freedom of choice and action from persons who are clothed with authority to restrain us—*government*, in short. Or to approach the subject from the opposite angle, we enjoy *civil liberty* because of the restraints which government imposes upon our neighbors in our behalf [5] and *constitutional liberty* because of the constitutional restraints under which government itself operates when it seeks to impose restraints upon us.

Finally, *constitutional liberty* itself is of two kinds: first, that which results from *political* checks and balances and from the conceptions of governmental function which are at any particular period held by politicians—an *internal* check, as it were; and, second, that which results from the more specialized type of check and balance

---

[5] It is of *civil liberty* in this sense that Montesquieu was thinking when he wrote: "Liberty is the right of doing what the laws permit; and if a citizen could do what they forbid, he would be no longer possessed of liberty, because all his fellow citizens would have the same power." *Spirit of the Laws* (Nugent tr., ed. of 1766), I, xi, 4 (p. 220).

which we Americans term *judicial review*, and which is recorded in the prevalent constitutional law of a period. And it is this latter type of constitutional liberty which is here termed *juridical liberty*, and whose origins and transmutations furnish the central theme of this study.[6]

So much for the first word in our title—how about the opposed term, "government"? This too undergoes a change in meaning. Under the regime of judicial review as we know it in this country the legislative branch is *ipso facto* designated as the great potential menace to liberty, whereas in medieval England, the common nidus of Anglo-American political institutions, "the legislative branch,"—if by a sort of historian's license we may so term the Parliaments of the period—was the *protector* of liberty and the royal power was deemed to be the chief source of danger to it. How this reversal in the role of

[6] No better statement of the American credo on the subject of constitutional liberty is to be found than Webster's answer to Jackson's Protest Message of April 15, 1834:

"The first object of a free people is the preservation of their liberty; and liberty is only to be preserved by maintaining constitutional restraints and just divisions of political power. Nothing is more deceptive or more dangerous than the pretence of a desire to simplify government. The simplest governments are despotisms; the next simplest, limited monarchies; but all republics, all governments of law, must impose numerous limitations and qualifications of authority and give many positive and qualified rights. In other words, they must be subject to rule and regulation. This is the very essence of free political institutions. The spirit of liberty is, indeed, a bold and fearless spirit, but it is also a sharpsighted spirit. . . . It demands checks; it seeks for guards; it insists on securities; it entrenches itself behind strong defences, and fortifies itself with all possible care against the assaults of ambition and passion. . . . This is the nature of constitutional liberty; and this is our liberty, if we will rightly understand and preserve it." *Writings and Speeches* (National ed., 1905), VII, 122–23.

the legislative branch came about, and the ensuing changes in the conception of "legislative power" will supply, consequently, a minor, though complementary theme in the following pages.

CHAPTER II

ROMAN AND ENGLISH ORIGINS

According to the Positive School of Jurisprudence "law" is "a general expression for the particular commands of a *human* law-giver"; [1] and by the underlying theory of popular government the highest possible source of such commands is "the people." Both ideas are logically implied in the famous text of Justinian's *Institutes*, that "Whatever has pleased the prince has the force of law, inasmuch as . . . the Roman people have vested in him all their power and authority." [2] Throughout the Middle Ages there was great debate whether the power thus ceded by the people could be recovered. [3] The Constitution in

[1] Jeremy Bentham, as quoted in T. E. Holland, *Elements of Jurisprudence* (12th ed., 1916), 14. For further definitions of "positive law," see *ibid.*, 22–23; Westel Woodbury Willoughby, *Fundamental Concepts of Public Law* (1924), Chap. X.

[2] *Inst.* I, 2, 6: "*Quod principi placuit, legis habet vigorem, cum lege regia quae de ejus imperio lata est, populus ei et in eum, omne imperium suum et potestatem concessit.*" The source is Ulpian, *Dig.* I, 4, 1. The Romans always regarded the people as the source of the legislative power. "*Lex est, quod populus Romanus senatorio magistratu interrogante, veluti Consule, constituebat.*" *Inst.* I, 2, 4.

[3] The question was whether the *lex regia* effected an absolute alienation (*translatio*) of the legislative power to the emperor, or was a rev-

avouching itself to be at once *law*, *supreme law*, and an *ordinance of the People of the United States*, assumes that it could be, and had been.

But while the attribution of supremacy to our constitutions on the ground of their rootage in popular will has always sufficed for those provisions which provide the framework of government and the delegation and distribution of its powers, this was far from being the case originally as regards those constitutional provisions which define and protect the rights of person and of property—in short, bills of rights. Thus the Ninth Article of the national Bill of Rights stipulates that "the enumeration of certain rights in this Constitution shall not prejudice other *rights* not so enumerated." This language assumes that there are individual rights of so transcendent a character that they owe nothing to their recognition in written constitutions, but that, on the contrary, a written constitution which neglected to recognize them would be to that extent a defective, an incomplete instrument of government, and that this deficiency would have to be made good from some outside source. It is predicated that there are certain principles of right and justice which are entitled to prevail simply because of their own intrinsic excellence, and without regard to the attitude of those who wield the physical resources of the community.

So far, therefore, as the Constitution of the United States purported to be a muniment of human rights and liberties, its *legality* and its *supremacy* alike derived orig-

---

ocable delegation (*cessio*). The champions of popular sovereignty at the end of this period, like Marsiglio of Padua in his *Defensor Pacis*, took the latter view. See Otto Gierke, *Political Theories of the Middle Ages* (Maitland's tr., 1922), 150, notes 158, 159.

inally from belief in *a law superior to the will of any possible human governors or law-makers.* Whence came this idea of a "higher law"? Through what agencies did it find its way to America, to be wrought into the American system of constitutional law? What transformations has it undergone that are of particular interest in the history of our constitutional law? What is its status with us today? All of these are questions with which these pages will deal.

When President Coolidge declared in 1919 that "Men do not make laws, they do but discover them," [4] he was probably unaware that he was echoing Demosthenes' assertion of more than two thousand years earlier that, "Every law is a discovery, a gift of God, a precept of wise men." [5] Even earlier, Sophocles had put in Antigone's mouth an appeal to "the ancient and steadfast customs of the gods" against King Creon's edict that her brother Polynices, whom Creon had slain, should remain unburied. [6]

But it was Demosthenes' great contemporary Aristotle who seems first to have visioned the possibilities of this conception in institutional terms, as when he advised advocates that when they had "no case according to the law of the land," they should "appeal to the law of nature,"

---

[4] Calvin Coolidge, *Have Faith in Massachusetts* (1919), 4; John Dickinson, *Administrative Justice and the Supremacy of Law* (1927), 85–86n.

[5] Holland, *Elements of Jurisprudence,* 44, note 1. "If there be any primitive theory of the nature of law, it seems to be that laws are the utterance of some divine or heroic person who reveals . . . that which is absolutely right." Sir Frederick Pollock and Frederick W. Maitland, *History of English Law* (1895), I, xxviii.

[6] Holland, *Elements of Jurisprudence,* 32, note 4, citing Sophocles, *Antigone,* vv, 450 *et seq.*

and, quoting the *Antigone* of Sophocles, argue that "an unjust law is not a law." [7] Moreover, putting the question in his *Politics* whether the rule of law or the rule of an individual is preferable, Aristotle answered: "To invest the law then with authority is, it seems, to invest God and reason only; to invest a man is to introduce a beast, as desire is something bestial, and even the best of men in authority are liable to be corrupted by passion. We may conclude then that the law is reason without passion and hence is preferable to any individual." [8] Nearly two thousand years after Aristotle, the sense of this passage, condensed into the Englishman Harrington's famous phrase, "a government of laws and not of men," [9] was to find its way first into the Massachusetts constitution of 1780 and two decades later into Chief Justice Marshall's opinion in Marbury *v.* Madison.[10]

The traceable American tradition, however, both of civil liberty and of constitutional liberty, as I have earlier

[7] David George Ritchie, *Natural Rights* (1903), 30, citing Aristotle, *Rhetoric* I, 15, 1375, a, 27 *et seq.*

[8] Aristotle, *Politics* (Welldon tr., 1905), bk. III, 15–16, especially at 154. I have departed slightly from the translation at one or two points. It does not appear, however, that Aristotle himself accepted the view here stated, at any rate unqualifiedly. He seems in this chapter and the immediately preceding one to be summing up the debate between the advocates and opponents of monarchy, concluding with these words: "Such are practically the objections urged by the opponents of kingly government. It is possible however that the conditions supposed exist in some cases and not in others. . . ." Welldon, 157.

[9] James Harrington, *Oceana and Other Works* (1747), 37. "An empire of laws and not of men." *Ibid.*, 45, 240; see also *ibid.*, 49, 240, 257, 362, 369. Harrington ascribes the idea to Aristotle and Livy.

[10] *Declaration of Rights*, Art. 30; Francis Newton Thorpe (ed.), *American Charters, Constitutions, and Organic Laws* (1909); 1 Cranch 137, 163 (1803).

defined these terms, took its rise a considerable time after Aristotle. Its source is Cicero's effort to render into juristic idiom the Stoic conception of a universal order, a cosmos, based on a divine reason which directs alike the movements of the heavenly bodies and the conduct of good men.[11] In a passage in his essay *Concerning the Commonwealth* (*De Re Publica*) for which we are indebted to one of the Church Fathers—the preservative quality of a good style has rarely been exemplified more strikingly—Cicero describes "natural law (*lex naturalis*)" as "right reason, harmonious with nature, diffused among all," a law which "may not be derogated from nor abrogated," a law which "requires no interpreter, since all men are capable of understanding it, a law which is the same for Rome as for Athens, the same at one time as at another."[12]

But it is in his *Concerning the Laws* (*De Legibus*) that Cicero makes his most distinctive contribution. Identifying "right reason" with those qualities of human nature whereby "man is associated with the gods," he assigns the binding quality of the civil law itself to its being in harmony with the universal attributes of human nature. In the natural endowment of man, and especially in his

[11] On the doctrines of the Stoics, see Diogenes Laertius, *Lives and Opinions of Eminent Philosophers* (Yonge tr., 1853), bk. vii, "Zeno," cc. 53, 55, 66, 70, 72–73. "Again, they say that justice exists by nature, and not because of any definition or principle; just as law does, or right reason." *Ibid.*, c. 66. "The Stoics . . . thought of Nature or the Universe as a living organism, of which the material world was the body, and of which the Deity or the Universal Reason was the pervading, animating, and governing soul; and natural law was the rule of conduct laid down by this Universal Reason for the direction of mankind." Sir John Salmond, *Jurisprudence* (7th ed., 1924), 27. See also Holland, *Elements of Jurisprudence*, 33–34.

[12] Lactantius, *Div. Inst.* (Roberts and Donaldson tr., 1871), vi, 8, 370; see also *ibid.*, 24.

social traits, "is to be found," Cicero asserts, "the true source of laws and rights." And he later adds, "We are born for justice, and right is not a mere arbitrary construction of opinion, but an institution of nature." Hence justice is not, as the Epicureans claim, mere utility, for "that which is established on account of utility may for utility's sake be overturned." There is, in short, discoverable in the permanent elements of human nature itself a durable justice, one which transcends expediency, and the positive law must embody this if it is to claim the allegiance of the human reason.[13]

Ordinarily, moreover, human authority fulfills this requirement—this Cicero unquestionably holds. Hence his statement that "the laws are the foundation of the liberty which we enjoy; we all are the laws' slaves that we may be free." The reference is clearly to the civil law. And of like import is his assertion that "nothing is more conformable to right and to the order of nature than authority (*imperium*)," and the accompanying picture of the sway of law, in which the civil law becomes a part of the pattern of the entire fabric of universal order.[14] Yet that the formal law, and especially enacted law, may at times part company with "true law" and thereby lose its title to be considered law at all is implied by his entire position; nor, in fact, do we have to rely upon implication. "Not all things," he writes, "are necessarily just which are established by the civil laws and institutions of nations"; nor is "justice identical with obedience to the written laws." The vulgar, to be sure, are wont to apply the term "law" to whatever is "written, forbidding certain things and

---

[13] *De Leg.* (Müller, ed.), I, 5, 16; 10, 28; 15, 42.
[14] *Pro A. Cluentio Oratio*, c. 53, § 146; *De Leg.*, III, 1, 2–3.

commanding others"; but it is so only in a colloquial sense.
"If it were possible to constitute right simply by the commands of the people, by the decrees of princes, by the
adjudications of magistrates, then all that would be necessary in order to make robbery, adultery, or the falsifica-
tion of wills right and just would be a vote of the multitude." But "the nature of things" is not thus subject to
"the opinions and behests of the foolish." True law is "a
rule of distinction between right and wrong according to
nature"; and "any other sort of law not only ought not to
be regarded as law, it ought not to be called law." [15]

When, however, that which wears the appearance of
law is at variance with true law, what then is the remedy?
When he came to answer this question, certain Roman
procedural forms connected with the enactment of law
suggested to Cicero something strikingly akin to our own
institution of judicial review. It was a Roman practice to
incorporate in statutes a saving clause to the effect that
it was no purpose of the enactment to abrogate what was
sacrosanct or "*jus.*" In this way certain maxims, or "*leges
legum,*" as Cicero styles them, some of which governed
the legislative process itself, were erected into a species
of written constitution binding on the legislative power;
and more than once we find Cicero, in reliance on such
a clause, invoking *jus* against a statute. "What is it," he
inquires on one occasion, "that is not *jus?* . . . This saving clause (*adscriptio*) declares that it is something, otherwise it would not be provided for in all our laws. And I
ask you, if the people had commanded that I should be
your slave, or you mine, would that be validly enacted,
fixed, established?" On other occasions he points out that

[15] *De Leg.,* I, 15, 42; 6, 19; 16, 43–44; II, 5, 13; 6, 13.

it was within the power both of the augurs and of the senate to abrogate laws which had not been enacted *jure*, although here the reference appears to be to the procedure of legislation, and he gives instances of the exercise of these purgative powers. We also find him appealing in the senate on one occasion directly to *"recta ratio"* as against the *"lex scripta."* [16]

[16] See Brissonius (Barnabé Brisson), *De Formulis et Solemnibus Populi Romani Verbis* (Leipsic, 1754), Lib. 2, c. 19, 129-30. The work first appeared in 1583. The customary form of the saving clause was, *"Si quid sacri sanctique est, quod jus non sit rogari, ejus hac lege nihil rogatur."* In his *Pro Caecina Oratio*, Cicero gives a somewhat different form, taken from an enactment of Sulla: *"Si quid jus non debet rogari, ejus ea lege nihilum rogatum." Ibid.,* cc. 32-33. A variant on this form appears in his *Pro Domo Sua*, c. 40. On these occasions Cicero is relying on the saving clause; but in his *Pro Balbo* the shoe is on the other foot, and he there argues against the extension of such a clause to a certain treaty, that nothing can be *"sacrosanctum nisi quod populus plebesve sanxisset,"* whereas the treaty in question had been made by the senate. *Ibid.,* c. 14. Cicero himself suffered from "a new and previously unheard of use" of the clause by his enemy Clodius, who endeavored by affixing it to the law exiling Cicero and confiscating his property to render the confiscation irrepealable. For Cicero's argument against the possibility of thus clothing statutes with immortality, see *Epistolae*, III, 22; and Brissonius, *De Formulis*, p. 130. See further *De Leg.*, II, 7, 18; and 12, 31; also Brinton Coxe, *Judicial Power and Unconstitutional Legislation* (1893), 111, citing Sir William Smith, *Dictionary of Greek and Roman Antiquities* (1842), art. *lex*. My friend, Professor John Dickinson, lent me valuable aid in tracing down these anticipations by Cicero of judicial review. Cicero's anticipation of the modern use of the word *constitution* is even more striking: Referring to a mixed or balanced form of government, he says: "This constitution (*haec constitutio*) has a great measure of equability without which men can hardly remain free for any length of time"; and again: "Now that opinion of Cato becomes more certain that the constitution of the republic (*constitutionem rei publicae*) is the work of no single time or of no single man." Charles H. McIlwain, *Constitutionalism, Ancient and Modern* (Cornell Univ. Press, 1940), 27-28, citing *De Re. Pub.*, I, 45 (69).

Except for a single doubtful instance, there is no proof that Cicero's anticipations of judicial review ever actually came to the attention of the framers of the American constitutions,[17] although, taken along with Aristotle's similar suggestion, they serve to show how immediate, if not inevitable, is the step from the notion of a higher law entering into the municipal law to that of a recourse against the latter on the basis of the former. And if Cicero did not contribute to the establishment of judicial review directly, he at any rate did so indirectly through certain ideas which enter into the argumentative justification of that institution. One of these is his assertion that natural law requires no interpreter other than the individual himself, a notion which is still sometimes reflected in the contention of courts and commentators that unconstitutional statutes are unconstitutional per se, and not because of any authority attaching to the court that so pronounces them. Another is his description of the magistrate as "the law speaking (*magistratum legem esse loquentem, legem autem mutum magistratum*)." The sense of this passage from the *De Legibus* is reproduced 1,600 years later in Coke's *Reports* in the words, "*Judex est lex loquens*," and 200 years after that in Chief Justice Marshall's assertion in his opinion in Osborn *v.* the Bank, in 1824, that "Judicial

[17] In the notes for his argument in Rutgers *v.* Waddington, Mayor's Ct., New York City (1784), Hamilton included the following passage: "*Si leges duae aut si plures aut quot quot erunt conservari non possunt quia discrepent inter se ea maxime conservanda sunt quae ad maximas res pertinere videantur*," citing "*De In: L 4, No. 145.*" A. M. Hamilton, *Hamilton* (1910), 462. The passage is in fact from *De Inventione*, II, 49. The context casts doubt as to whether it was intended by Cicero in quite the sense for which Hamilton appears to have employed it.

power, as contradistinguished from the power of the laws, has no existence." [18]

Of other features of the Ciceronian version of natural law, outstanding is his conception of human equality: "There is no one thing so like or so equal to one another as all of us are to one another. And if the corruption of custom and the variation of opinion did not induce an imbecility of minds and turn them aside from the course of nature, no one would more resemble himself than all men would resemble all men. Therefore, whatever definition we give to man will be applicable to the entire race." [19] Not only was this good Stoic teaching, it was the inescapable consequence of Cicero's notion of the constancy of the distinctive attributes of human nature, those which supply the foundation of natural law.

With respect to certain other elements of the doctrine of natural law as it entered American constitutional theory, the assignment of credit cannot be made so confidently. The notion of popular sovereignty, of a social contract, and of a contract between governors and governed are all foreshadowed by Cicero with greater or less

[18] *De Leg.*, III, 1, 2–3; Calvin's Case, 4 Co. 1 (1609); 9 Wheat. 738, 866 (1824).

[19] *De Leg.*, I, 10, 12–28, 33. "There is no conception which is more fundamental to the Aristotelian theory of society than the notion of the natural inequality of human nature. . . . There is no change in political theory so startling in its completeness as the change from the theory of Aristotle to the later philosophical view represented by Cicero and Seneca. Over against Aristotle's view of the natural inequality of human nature we find set the theory of the natural equality of human nature. . . . There is only one possible definition for all mankind, reason is common to all." A. J. Carlyle, *A History of Mediaeval Political Theory* (1927), I, 7–8.

distinctness.[20] The notion of a state of nature, however, is missing, to be supplied later by Seneca and the early Church Fathers, the latter of whom located their primitive polity in the Garden of Eden before the Fall. It is Seneca too who corrects Cicero's obtuseness, later repeated by the signers of the Declaration of Independence, to the contradiction between the idea of the equality of man and the institution of slavery; and in this respect his views were subsequently ratified by certain of the great Roman jurists. Ulpian, writing at the close of the second century, asserted unqualifiedly that "by the law of nature all men are born free," words which were repeated in the *Institutes* three hundred years after that. Natural law, we observe, is already putting forth the stem of natural rights that is ultimately to dwarf and overshadow it.[21]

The apostle to the Teutonic world of the Ciceronian conception of "true law" as "right reason" was an English cleric, John of Salisbury, whose *Policraticus*, or *Statesman's Book*, was the earliest systematic work on politics of the Middle Ages. "There are certain precepts of the law," John writes, "which have perpetual necessity, having the force of law among all nations and which absolutely cannot be broken." This is the Ciceronian doctrine of natural law in a sentence; but the problem to

---

[20] *De Re Pub.*, I, 25, 26, 32; III, 3, 13, 31. Editors also assign to the same chapter, preserved by St. Augustine, the following: "*Quid est res publica nisi res populi? Res ergo communis, res utique civitatis.*" St. Augustine, *Epistles*, 138, 10, and *De Civitate Dei*, v, 18. It is evident that the notion of popular sovereignty in the sense of unlimited legislative power cannot be attributed to Cicero. See also *De Re Pub.*, III, 3.

[21] *Inst.* I, 2, 2; Carlyle, *History of Mediaeval Political Theory*, I, 23–25, 47, 117, 134, 144–46.

whose solution John brought the doctrine was very different from the one which Cicero had foremost in mind. Legislation as it was known in the days of the later Republic and under the Empire was at an end; rulership was in the hands of military chieftains and was essentially personal. That which took the place of law at this period and for long afterward was immemorial custom, or what claimed to be such; and its relation to rulership was that of a check rather than an instrument. John's endeavor accordingly is to equate so far as possible *rex* with *lex*. Particularly illuminating are those passages in which he endeavors to draw the teeth of certain troublesome texts of Justinian's *Digest* and *Institutes*, especially that which asserts that the prince is *"legibus solutus,"* and the one quoted earlier in these pages, which declares that "what has pleased the prince, . . . has the force of law." It is not true, John asserts, that the prince is absolved from the obligations of the law "in the sense that it is lawful for him to do unjust acts," but only in the sense that his character should guarantee his doing equity "not through fear of the penalties of the law but through love of justice." And as to "the will of the prince," in respect of public matters, he says, "the prince may not lawfully have any will of his own apart from that which the law or equity enjoins, or calculation of the common interest requires." Indeed the very title *rex* is derived from doing right, that is, acting in accordance with law (*recte*).[22]

[22] John Dickinson, *The Statesman's Book of John of Salisbury* (1927), 7, 33, 335–36. The notion that the prince is subject to the law is, of course, much older than the *Policraticus*. Stobaeus credits Solon with saying that "that was the best government where the subjects obeyed their prince, and the prince the laws." Notice also Fortescue's quotation from Diodorus Siculus, that "the kings of Egypt originally

The importance of all this is that in arguing in this way John foreshadowed, even though he did not altogether succeed in formulating it, the distinctive contribution of the Middle Ages to modern political science, and especially to American political science, the notion that all political authority is *intrinsically limited authority*— limited, especially, by the end for which it was created. Conceding the principle, however, an exigent question of a practical nature arises: how are such limitations to be ascertained and enforced? On the Continent this question went unanswered, but in John's own country and the mother country of our own institutions it furnished the main stimulus to constitutional development for five centuries.[23]

While as a general thing historical parallels are apt to prove more of a hindrance than a help to real comprehension of the past, yet when they are associated with the history of an idea the case is often otherwise. For ideas have, in a sense, a life of their own, an internal vigor which is capable of calling forth suitable institutions to embody them, and furthermore a particular idea is apt to display a certain constancy of preference in this respect in whatever environment it is encountered. Certain it is that the contribution of medieval England to the American theory

---

did not live in such a licentious manner as other kings, whose will was their law: but were subject to the same law, in common with their subjects, and esteemed themselves happy in such a conformity to the laws." Sir John Fortescue, *De Laudibus Legum Angliae* (Amos tr., 1825), c. 13.

[23] It ought perhaps to be mentioned that John's own answer to the above question, so far as he attempted one, was the doctrine of tyrannicide. Citing the example of Sisera and Holofernes, he declared that to kill a tyrant was "not merely lawful, but right and just." Dickinson, *The Statesman's Book of John of Salisbury*, lxxii–iv.

of Liberty versus Government exhibits some striking similarities to the strictly American phase of the subject. There is to begin with a fundamental document, Magna Carta, to symbolize the subordination of political authority to law. Then ensues the slow absorption of this document into judge-made law, a process which is attended by the projection of a portion of the latter into the status of a higher law of liberty. Lastly, this higher law of liberty becomes an avowed professional mystery—the arcana of the Bench and Bar. At the same time there is a minor parallel between the roles played in the two cases by commentators.

There was a time not so many years ago when scholars took a scandalous delight in writing down the Great Charter as "a feudal," "a reactionary document." The sound residuum that remains from this often frothy criticism is that *Magna Carta* was not at first all that *Magna Charta* eventually became, and indeed became quite early.[24] For the history of American constitutional law and theory no part of Magna Carta can compare in importance with chapter twenty-nine: "No free man shall be taken or im-

[24] The leader of the sceptics was Professor Edward Jenks, who contributed to the *Independent Review* for 1904 an article entitled "The Myth of Magna Carta." In an excellent article bearing the same title, which appears in the September, 1947, *Harvard Law Review* (vol. 60, pp. 1060–91), Professor Max Radin overwhelms the sceptics foot and horse. The article lists references to the Charter in statutes and Year Books, and those by chroniclers, poets, and others. It shows that while Shakespeare did not mention the Charter yet it had by no means dropped out of popular knowledge and regard even at the end of Elizabeth's reign. One point neglected by Professor Radin is that the diminished attention given the Charter in legal sources in the latter part of the period reviewed by him was due to its very success in being absorbed into the common law. See note 33 *infra*.

prisoned or deprived of his freehold or of his liberties or
free customs, or outlawed, or exiled, or in any manner
destroyed, nor shall we go upon him, nor shall we send
upon him, except by a legal judgment of his peers or by
the law of the land." [25]

Our present interest in this famous text is centered upon
its opening phrase, "no free man *(nullus liber homo)*." Although the words *liber homo* may have designated at
first few outside the vassal class, in this as in other respects
the Charter early manifested capacity for growth. The
re-issue of 1225, "the Great Charter" of history, was contemporaneously described as conceding their liberties alike
"to people and to populace *(tam populo quam plebi)*";
and a quarter-century later we find the term "common
liberties" being used to characterize the subject matter
of the Charter. Even more striking is Bracton's—Henry
of Bratton's—term for it, *"constitutio libertatis,"* words
which consolidate all particular liberties into *one* liberty.[26]
Nor was Bracton speaking merely casually. For his great
work *Concerning the Laws and Customs of England (De
Legibus et Consuetudinibus Angliae)* is shot through with
John of Salisbury's conception of limited monarchical
power, doctrine which Bracton compressed into the axiom
that "the King ought to be under no man, but under

[25] *"Nullus liber homo capiatur vel imprisonetur aut disseisietur de
libero tenemento suo vel libertatibus vel liberis consuetudinibus suis
aut utlagetur aut exuletur aut aliquo modo destruatur nec super eum
ibimus nec super eum mittemus, nisi per legale judicium parium suorum
vel per legem terrae."* Compare c. 29 of the issue of 1225 and c. 39 of
the original issue. It is the 1225 issue which "became the Great Charter
of English law," also called *"Magna Charta."*

[26] Radin, *loc. cit.;* Charles Howard McIlwain, "Magna Carta and
Common Law," in *Magna Carta Commemoration Essays* (Malden ed.,
1917), 156–60, 171.

God and the law (*sub Deo et lege*), for the law makes the King." [27]

Nor did Magna Carta develop solely along one dimension. As the range of classes and interests brought under its protection widened, its quality as higher law binding in some sense upon government in all its phases steadily strengthened until it becomes possible to look upon it in the fourteenth century as something very like a written constitution in the modern understanding. By his *confirmatio cartarum* of 1297, Edward I ordered all "justices, sheriffs, mayors, and other ministers, which under us and by us have the laws of our land to guide," to treat the Great Charter as "common law" in all pleas before them. Any judgment contrary to the Great Charter or the Charter of the Forest was to be "holden for naught"; and all archbishops and bishops were to pronounce "the sentence of the Great Excommunication against all those that by deed, aid, or counsel" proceeded "contrary to the aforesaid charters" or in any point transgressed them. The conception of Magna Carta as higher

---

[27] *De Legibus et Consuetudinibus Angliae* (Twiss ed., 1854), f. 5b. In these words we have again the characteristic medieval idea of all authority as deriving from the law and as, therefore, limited by it. Bracton's own words, it will be noted, are strongly reminiscent of John of Salisbury, and elsewhere the similarity becomes even more striking. The king's power, he writes, is the power of justice, not of injustice. So long as he does justice, the king is the vicar of God; but when he turns aside to injustice, he is the minister of the devil. Indeed, he is called "king" (*rex*) from "ruling well" (*regendo*), not from "reigning" (*regnando*). "Let him therefore, temper his power by law, which is the bridle of power . . . likewise is nothing so appropriate to empire as to live according to the laws, and to submit the princedom to law is greater than empire." *Ibid.*, f. 107b. But Bracton's position is by no means free of ambiguity. See the book review which I give in Appendix I to this volume.

law reached its culmination in the reign of Edward III. Of the thirty-two royal confirmations of the Charter noted by Sir Edward Coke, fifteen occurred in this reign; and near the end of it, in 1368, to the normal form of confirmation the declaration was added by statute that any statute passed contrary to Magna Carta *"soit tenuz p'nul,"* words which seem clearly to have been addressed to the royal officials, including the judges.[28]

Such were the outstanding features of the English constitution as it existed under the later Plantagenet and the early Lancastrian monarchs. It is interesting to reflect that this constitution was the common ancestor of both the British and the American constitutions of five hundred years later, and that it was the latter which bore much the stronger resemblance to the parent institution. It is true that the role sustained by Parliament in those earlier times as defender of Magna Carta presents a superficial contrast to American constitutional arrangements, but when it is more closely scrutinized, this tends to disappear. *Functionally*, these early Parliaments for the most part were not *lawmaking* bodies at all, for law was still generally conceived as something existing independently of human authority and so as something not enacted but declared, and especially was this true as to law governing *meum et tuum*.[29] Indeed, Magna Carta itself was by its own profession a *declaration* of pre-existing rights. To

[28] George Burton Adams and H. Morse Stephens, *Select Documents of English History* (1911), 86–87; 42 Edw. III, c. 1 (1368); 1 *Stat. Realm* 388 (1368); 3 *Co. Inst.* III; also 1 *ibid.*, 81.

[29] The leading work on this subject is Charles Howard McIlwain's path-making *High Court of Parliament and Its Supremacy* (Yale Univ. Press, 1910).

have characterized it as creative would have been to stigmatize it as an act of usurpation.

Also in point, as foreshadowing the parallel development of American constitutional law four centuries later, is the fact that the day came when Parliament's guardianship of Magna Carta yielded precedence for a period to the guardianship of the ordinary courts over the common law. For this there were several causes, two of which were of outstanding importance: first, the enfeeblement of Parliament through the almost complete destruction of the old nobility in the Wars of the Roses; second, the immense enhancement of the prestige and social influence of the ordinary courts through the rise of a learned bar, of which the judges were the nucleus, though only the nucleus. At a time when people did not know from day to day whether Lancaster or York sat on the throne, the common-law courts continued for the most part in the discharge of their proper business. The result was that, as Englishmen recognized in the daily practice of the courts an actual realization of most that Magna Carta had symbolized, they transferred to the common law as a whole the worship which they had so long reserved more especially for the Charter. The common law, infused with the principles of Magna Carta, came to be regarded as *higher law*, and, without losing its quality as *positive law*, law known to and administered by the royal courts.[30]

[30] See *Paston Letters* (Fenn ed., 1873), *passim*. Magna Carta is "part of the common law and the ancient law of this kingdom," 2 Hansard, *Parliamentary History*, 333 (1628). "The King cannot dispense with Magna Charta, which is incorporated into the Common Law." 6 Comyn, *Digest* (Dublin ed., 1793), 35 tit. *Praerogative*, D. 7, citing 2 *Rol.* 115.

Writing with this period particularly in mind, Father Figgis says: "The Common Law is pictured invested with a halo of dignity peculiar to the embodiment of the deepest principles and to the highest expression of human reason and of the law of nature implanted by God in the heart of man. As yet men are not clear that an Act of Parliament can do more than declare the Common Law. It is the Common Law which men set up as an object of worship. The Common Law is the perfect ideal of law; for it is natural reason developed and expounded by a collective wisdom of many generations. . . . Based on long usage and almost supernatural wisdom, its authority is above, rather than below that of Acts of Parliament or royal ordinances, which owe their fleeting existence to the caprice of the King or to the pleasure of councillors, which have a merely material sanction and may be repealed at any moment." [31]

[31] John Neville Figgis, *Divine Right of Kings* (2d ed., 1914), 228–30. "The common law is the absolute perfection of reason." 2 *Co. Inst.* 179. The common law, "having a principle of growth and progress in itself . . . is already . . . the most complete and admirable system of law— the most healthy and vigorous in its principles, the most favorable to civil liberty, standing the nearest to the divine law, and the best fitted to be the auxiliary and helper of religion itself in the government of individual men and of human society—that has ever existed on earth." John Dewey Barnard, *Discourse on the Life, Character, and Public Services of Ambrose Spencer* (1849), 52. "It has been my amusement for many years past, as far as I have had leisure, to examine the systems of all the legislators, ancient and modern, fantastical and real . . . , and the result . . . is a settled opinion that the liberty, the unalienable, indefeasible rights of men, the honor and dignity of human nature, the grandeur and glory of the public, and the universal happiness of individuals, were never so skillfully and successfully consulted as in that most excellent monument of human art, the common law of England." John Adams, *Life and Works* (1851), III, 440. Adams was writing in 1763.

Foremost of these fifteenth-century panegyrists of the common law was Sir John Fortescue, who had been Henry VI's Chief Justice and had followed his royal master into exile. In his nostalgic *In Praise of the Laws of England* (*De Laudibus Legum Angliae*), a work which links Bracton with Coke, Sir John describes the laws of England as repelling that maxim of tyranny, "*quod principi placuit, legis habet vigorem,*" "which the laws of France admit," and as declaring "in all cases . . . in favor of liberty, the gift of God to man in his creation."[32] Yet this divine donation, it appears from other pages of the *De Laudibus*, is not conferred upon mankind directly as Cicero and John of Salisbury after him had taught, but indirectly through the judges. Indeed, Sir John asserts dogmatically the complete identity of "perfect justice" with "legal justice," the justice of the law courts. It is not that mankind in general can have *no* comprehension of legal learning, but such as they have is superficial, comparable with that which they have of "faith, love, charity, the sacraments, and God's commandments," while leaving "other mysteries in Divinity to those who preside in the Church."[33]

[32] Amos ed. (1825), c. 42, p. 157. This edition follows Francis Gregor's translation of 1775—sometimes too faithfully. At the close of chapter 34, p. 128, Fortescue is made by both editors to say: "It is not a restraint, but rather a liberty to govern a people by the just regularity of a *political* government, or rather right reason." No equivalent of the last four words appears in the Latin original. All previous editions have today been superseded by that of S. B. Chrimes (Cambridge Univ. Press, 1942). I have gathered from a casual examination of it that it says nothing that should require me to recast what I have already said.

[33] *Ibid.*, c. 4, p. 11; c. 8, p. 20. It should be noted that Fortescue does not mention Magna Carta in *De Laudibus*, although he does, according

Nor is the case of the ruler himself substantially different from that of the generality of his subjects in this respect. Hence "the Chancellor," who is Sir John's mouthpiece, is made to say: "My Prince, there will be no occasion for you to search into the arcana of our laws with such tedious application and study. . . . It will not be convenient by severe study, or at the expense of the best of your time, to pry into nice points of law: such matters may be left to your judges and counsel . . . ; furthermore, you will pronounce judgment in the courts by others than in person, it being not customary for the Kings of England to sit in court or pronounce judgment themselves (*proprio ore nullus regum Angliae judicium proferre usus est*). I know very well the quickness of your apprehension and the forwardness of your parts; but for that expertness in the laws which is requisite for judges the studies of twenty years (*viginti annorum lucubrationes*) barely suffice." [34]

---

to Professor Radin, "in his judgments in the Year Books . . . as does the great Littleton." 60 *Harvard Law Review*, 1083.

[34] *De Laud.*, c. 8. The colloquy thus imagined by Fortescue was enacted in solemn earnest 130 years later. On Sunday morning, November 10, 1608, Coke and "all the judges of England, and the Barons of the Exchequer" faced James I at Hampton Court to confute the notion which had been instilled in him by Archbishop Bancroft that, inasmuch as the judges were but his delegates, he was entitled to decide cases in his own person. "The judges informed the King," Coke records, "that no King after the Conquest assumed to himself to give any judgment in any cause whatsoever, which concerned the administration of justice within this realm, but these were solely determined in the courts of justice. . . ." To this the King answered that "he thought the law was founded on reason, and that he and others had reason, as well as the Judges"; but Coke pointed out the fallacy of this view in the following words: "True it was, that God had endowed his Majesty with excellent science, and great endowments of nature; but his Majesty was not

Thus the king is under the law, which only the judges know—he is, in short, under the judges. *English liberty as an effective restraint on authority has its source in a professional, a craft mystery.* And to the same source, if we are to believe Fortescue, was to be traced the reason why fifteenth-century Englishmen wore "good woollens," and had always "great abundance" of "all sorts of flesh and fish," and drank "no water, unless at certain times, upon a religious score and by way of doing penance." [35] One is led to recall the idyllic pictures that have often been painted of the American Way of Life and of its dependence upon American constitutional liberty as conceived by a certain section of the American bar.

But how did ideas which attained fruition in fifteenth-century England become the fountainhead of the stream of American constitutionalism? Through what agency or agencies and in what circumstances was the transference effected, across three centuries and the wide Atlantic? The question is the more intriguing by reason of the fact that throughout the 140 years of the Tudor monarchy the system which the *De Laudibus* depicted with such loving admiration was largely in abeyance, a condition of af-

---

learned in the laws of his realm of England, and causes which concern the life, or inheritance, or goods, or fortunes of his subjects are not to be decided by natural reason, but by the artificial reason and judgment of the law, which law is an act which requires long study and experience, before that a man can attain to the cognizance of it; and that the law was the golden met-wand and measure to try the causes of the subjects; and which protected his Majesty in safety and peace." "The King," the report continues, "was greatly offended," saying that, "then he should be under the law, which was treason to affirm," to which Coke responded in Bracton's words: "*Quod Rex non debet esse sub homine, sed sub Deo et lege.*" Prohibitions del Roy, 12 Co. 63–65 (1609).

[35] *De Laud.*, c. 36.

fairs curiously symbolized by Shakespeare's failure to so much as mention the Great Charter in his *King John*. And this is only a part of the story, for when the medieval conception of the relation of law to political authority did finally issue once more into the light of day early in the seventeenth century it was primarily to serve the purposes of English political controversy and to meet the challenge of opposed conceptions.

The Tudor monarchy made one outstanding contribution to the existing stock of political concepts. It revived the idea, which harks back to the popular assemblies of Greece and Rome and finds expression in Justinian's *Institutes*, that *law made by human beings can be of the highest obligation*. The outstanding achievement of the Tudors was the creation out of hand of a new ecclesiastical constitution for the realm, a work which was accomplished mainly by resort to the forms of parliamentary enactment. The consequence of this procedure for political thought is stated by Professor Maitland in the following words: "Throughout the Middle Ages there was at least one limitation set to temporal sovereignty; it had no power in spiritual matters. . . . But now statutes have gone to the very root of religion. . . . Thus statute has given the most conclusive proof of its power." [36]

[36] Frederick W. Maitland, *The Constitutional History of England* (Cambridge Univ. Press, 1908), 254.

"In the last session of the Reformation Parliament in 1536," writes Professor McIlwain, "two remarkable statutes were enacted truly revolutionary in character, the Statute of Uses . . . and the act transferring to the Crown the property of the lesser monasteries. Both these acts involve an invasion of private right by parliament almost, if not entirely, without precedent before 1536 and far more revolutionary than the Statute of Proclamations enacted by a subsequent parliament three years later, which has been called 'the English *Lex Regia*' and termed even by Maitland 'the most extraordinary act in the Statute

Nor did this lesson escape contemporary observers of the events on which it is based. The words of Sir Thomas Smith in his *Commonwealth of England* (*De Republica Anglorum*), which was published in 1589, offer conclusive testimony in this connection: "The most high and absolute power of the realme of Englande, consisteth in the Parliament. . . . That which is doone by this consent is called firme, stable, and *sanctum*, and is taken for lawe. The Parliament abrogateth olde lawes, maketh newe. . . . And to be short, all that ever the people of Rome might do either in *centuriatis comitiis* or *tributis*, the same may be doone by the Parliament of Englande which representeth and hath the power of the whole realme, both the head and the body. For everie Englishman is entended to bee there present, either in person or by procuration and attornies." [37] Clearly the author of this passage was not far from the notion of a legally un-

---

Book' (*The Constitutional History of England*, p. 253). These two statutes of 1536 therefore mark an important early stage in the developments which led in the course of time to the constitutional doctrine of parliament's omnipotence and the modern theory of legislative sovereignty." Charles H. McIlwain, *Constitutionalism, Ancient and Modern* (rev. ed.; Cornell Univ. Press, 1947), 170.

[37] Alston ed. (1906), bk. II, c. 1. In the preamble to the statute of 1534 concerning Peter's Pence and papal dispensations, Smith is anticipated: "It standeth therefore with natural Equity and good Reason, that in all and every such laws human made within this Realm, or induced into this Realm by the said Sufferance, Consents and Custom, your Royal Majesty, and your Lords Spiritual and Temporal, and Commons, *representing the whole State of your Realm*, in this your most high Court of Parliament, have *full Power and Authority*, not only to dispense *the said Laws, and every of them,* . . . [but also] *to abrogate, annul, amplify or diminish, as it shall be seen unto your Majesty, and the Nobles and Commons of your Realm present in your Parliament, meet and convenient* for the Wealth of your Realm." McIlwain, *Constitutionalism* (rev. ed.), 172. Coke, on the other hand, regards the bulk of the law of his time, both common and statute, as unalterable. 2 *Co. Inst.* 187.

limited lawmaking authority, the idea which today lies at the basis of the British constitution.

So—to repeat the question how did England's medieval constitution become the fountainhead of the American constitutional tradition?—the explanation is to be found in the first instance in the attempt of the early Stuarts to appropriate to the king alone powers which their predecessors had ventured to exercise only in association with Parliament, and in the role played by Sir Edward Coke in opposing these pretensions with a learning that was immense and which its possessor did not hesitate to embroider to suit his purpose. No one would contend that the tradition which Coke passed on to the founders of the American constitutional system suffered any diminution or attenuation at his hands.

Coke's war upon Stuart pretensions falls into two periods: first, that of his two chief justiceships and, secondly, that of his membership of Parliament. In the former period we find him seizing every opportunity to assert the doctrine that the royal prerogative was a common-law concept, and as such subject to judicial delimitation; [38] and in the famous case of Dr. Bonham, decided in 1610, he advanced like doctrine with respect to Parliament's power. Holding that the London College of Physicians was not entitled under the act of Parliament which it invoked in justification to compel Bonham to pay money into its own coffers for practicing medicine in the city without its license, Coke said: "And it appears in our books, that in many cases, the common law will controul acts of parliament, and sometimes adjudge them to be utterly void:

[38] See especially The Case of Proclamations, 12 Rep. 74 (1610); also note 34 *supra*.

for when an act of parliament is against common right and reason, or repugnant, or impossible to be performed, the common law will controul it and adjudge such act to be void . . . *iniquum est aliquem suae rei esse judicem.*" [39]

The first question to arise on this language is as to the meaning of the expression "common right and reason." Undoubtedly Coke is here referring to "that artificial reason and judgment of the law" of which he regarded Bench and Bar as the especial custodians. His employment of these terms is, however, by no means the narrowly official and precisionist one that it would probably have been a hundred years before. Early in the sixteenth century the author of *Doctor and Student,* possibly voicing the suspicion of the Tudor epoch toward principles restrictive of governmental authority, had taken pains to explain that the term "law of nature" "is not used among them that be learned in the laws of England." [40] The

[39] 8 Co. 118a (1610). The best comment on the dictum is to be found in McIlwain, *High Court of Parliament and Its Supremacy,* Chap. IV, and Theodore F. T. Plucknett, "Bonham's Case and Judicial Review," 40 *Harvard Law Review,* 30 ff. (1926). Lord Chancellor Ellesmere's charge that Coke had the support of only one judge and that three others were against him seems to be refuted both by Coke's and by Brownlow's report of the case. Apparently only three judges participated, and all agreed with Coke's statement. The case is cited by Chief Justice Taft in his opinion for the Court in Tumey v. Ohio, where a similar issue was presented. 273 U.S. 510, 524 (1927).

[40] Christopher St. Germain, *Doctor and Student* (Muchall ed., 1787), 12–13. Suspicion of ecclesiastical domination is given by Pollock as the reason for the reluctance of the sages of the common law before the Reformation to refer expressly to the laws of nature. Sir Frederick Pollock, *Expansion of the Common Law* (1904), 112–13. Fortescue, however, evinced no such reluctance. Bryce notes that both Yelverton and Lord Chancellor Stillington, who held office under Edward IV, referred to the law of nature. James Bryce, *Studies in History and*

point of view revealed by Coke and his associates contemporaneously with Bonham's Case is very different, as his summary of the argument that same year in Calvin's Case by the chief legal lights of England demonstrates: "1. That ligeance or obedience of the subject to the Sovereign is due by the law of nature: 2. That this law of nature is part of the laws of England: 3. That the law of nature was before any judicial or municipal law in the world: 4. That the law of nature is immutable, and cannot be changed." He then recites in support of these propositions the following quaint argument: "The law of nature is that which God at the time of creation of the nature of man infused into his heart, for his preservation and direction; and this is *lex aeterna*, the moral law, called also the law of nature. And by this law, written with the finger of God in the heart of man, were the people of God a long time governed before the law was written by Moses, who was the first reporter or writer of law in the world. . . . And Aristotle, nature's Secretary Lib. 5. Æthic. saith that *jus naturale est, quod apud omnes homines eandem habet potentiam*. And herewith doth agree Bracton lib. 1. cap. 6. and Fortescue cap. 8. 12. 13. and 16. *Doctor and Student*, cap. 2. and 4." [41]

The receptive attitude here evinced toward natural-law ideas, of which a fresh influx from the Continent was

---

Jurisprudence (1901), 601. Pollock himself adds: "It is not credible that a doctrine which pervaded all political speculation in Europe, and was assumed as a common ground of authority by the opposing champions of the Empire and the Papacy, should have been without influence among learned men in England." Bryce, *loc. cit. supra.* See also Sir Frederick Pollock, "History of the Law of Nature" in his *Essays in the Law* (1922), 157; J. Lawrence Lowell, *Government of England* (1908), 480–88.   [41] 7 Co. 1 4b, 12a–12b (1610).

already setting in, is a matter of profound importance. In the great constitutional struggle with the Stuarts it enabled Coke to build upon Fortescue, whose conception of liberty is shot through with natural-law implications, and it enabled Locke to build in turn upon Coke. It made allies of fifteenth-century legalism and seventeenth-century rationalism, and the alliance then struck has continued, now more, now less vital, in American constitutional law and theory.

And this brings us to a second question, that of Coke's meaning when he speaks of "controuling" an act of Parliament and "adjudging such act to be void." When the Supreme Court of the United States pronounces an act of Congress "void," it ordinarily means void *ab initio*, because beyond the power of Congress to enact, and it furthermore generally implies that the Court would similarly dispose of any further act of the same tenor. Was Coke laying claim to any such sweeping power for the ordinary courts as against acts of Parliament?

One thing seems to be assured: Coke was not asserting simply a rule of statutory construction which owed its force to the assumed intention of Parliament as it would today, although the statute involved in Bonham's Case was also construed from that point of view. At the very least, he deemed himself to be enforcing a rule of construction of statutes of higher intrinsic validity than any act of Parliament as such. Does this, on the other hand, necessarily signify that he regarded the ordinary courts as the *final* authoritative interpreters of such rule of construction?

There may have been a period when Coke, in view of the threatened deadlock between the king and the houses of Parliament, dreamed of giving the law to both through the mouths of the judges. Otherwise it is difficult to account for such criticisms as that voiced by Lord Chancellor Ellesmere, the accumulation of which became a material factor in forcing Coke's retirement from the bench six years later. But this would not mean that he regarded the ordinary courts as capable of giving the law to the "High Court of Parliament" in its capacity as a *law-declaring body*, when the latter was in position to exercise its jurisdiction. Indeed, his last years were especially devoted to asserting the competence of Parliament in this respect. For while the dictum uncovers one of the indispensable premises of the doctrine of judicial review, the other, that which rests on the principle of separation of powers, Coke lacked. This, of course, is a matter to be treated later.[42]

[42] In this connection the dictum should be compared with Coke's much later words in 4 *Inst.* 37: "I had it of Sir Thos. Gawdye, Knight, a grave and reverend judge of the King's bench, who lived at that time, that Henry VIII commanded him to attend the chief justices and to know whether a man that was forthcoming might be attainted for high treason by Parliament and never called to his answer. The judges answered that it was a dangerous question, and that the High Court of Parliament ought to give examples to inferior courts for proceeding according to justice, and no inferior court could do the like, and they thought that the High Court of Parliament would never do it. But being by the express commandment of the King and pressed by the said earl to give a direct answer, they said that if he be attainted by Parliament, it could not come in question afterwards, whether he were called or not to answer. And albeit their opinion was according to law, yet might they have made a better answer, for by the statutes of Magna Carta, Cap. 29, 5 Edw. III Cap. 9, and 28 Edw. III Cap. 5, no man ought to be condemned without answer, etc., which they might have certified but *facta tenent multa quae fieri prohibentur;* the act of attainder being passed by Parliament did bind, as they resolved." *Practically* this position is not so very different from that of Blackstone, but *theoretically* it

Approved by Lord Chief Justice Holt as late as 1701,[43] although in considerably diluted form, the dictum presently found its way into the digests and abridgments of the time, and it was from works such as these that James Otis took it in 1761 when, in the famous Writs of Assistance case he fired the opening gun in the controversy that led to the Revolution. John Adams' summary of Otis' argument reads as follows: "As to acts of Parliament. An act against the Constitution is void: an Act against natural Equity is void: and if an Act of Parliament should be made, in the very words of the petition, it would be void. The Executive Courts must pass such Acts into disuse.— 8 Rep. 118, from Viner." "Then and there," exclaims Adams, "the child Independence was born." He might well have added that then and there American constitutional law was born, for Otis' contention goes beyond Coke's: an ordinary court may traverse the *specifically*

---

is. For while Coke admits the power of Parliament to control the lower courts he does not admit that Parliament's erroneous precedents unmake Fundamental Law.

[43] 12 Mod. 678 (1701). Though there is no reference in Day *v.* Savadge to Bonham's Case, Chief Justice Hobart's words in the former are doubtless an echo: "Even an Act of Parliament, made against Natural Equity, as to make a Man Judge in his own Cause, is void in itself; for *jura naturae sunt immutabilia* and they are *leges legum.*" Hobart, 85 (1614). In 1636 Chief Justice Finch surpassed the dictum in dogmatic assertion of the legal limits on Parliament's powers. "Therefore Lawes positive, which are directly contrary to the former [the law of reason] lose their force, and are no Lawes at all. As those which are contrary to the law of Nature." *Law* (1636), bk. I, c. 6, quoted by Dean Pound, "Common Law and Legislation," 21 *Harvard Law Review*, 391–92 (1908). In Ship-Money Case, Finch advanced a similar doctrine in defense of the royal prerogative. "No act of parliament can bar a king of his regality. . . . Therefore acts of parliament to take away his royal power in defence of the kingdom are void." Maitland, *The Constitutional History of England*, 299.

enacted will of Parliament, and its condemnation is final.[44]

In 1616 Coke, who had three years earlier been transferred from the Common Pleas to the King's Bench, was dismissed as judge altogether. Four years later he was elected to the House of Commons, and there at once assumed the leadership of the growing opposition to the Stuarts. In 1625 Charles succeeded James, and in 1627 occurred the arbitrary arrest by royal order of the Five Knights, giving rise in Parliament to the great Inquest on the Liberties of the Subject, and eventually to the framing of the Petition of Right.[45] In all these proceedings the leading role fell to Coke, and their general tendency is made clear in the quaint words of Sir Benjamin Rudyard, who expressed his great gratification to see "that good, old, decrepid law of Magna Charta, which hath been so long kept in and lain bed-rid, as it were . . . walk abroad again."

Coke's main objective was still to curb the royal prerogative, but the terms in which he expressed himself assert also the existence of constitutional limits to Parliament's power as well. Especially significant are his remarks on the clause "saving the sovereign power" of the king which was at first attached to the Petition by the Lords. The question arising, "what is Sovereign power," a member quoted Bodin to the effect "that it is free from any conditions"; whereupon Coke arose and said: "This is *magnum in parvo*. . . . I know that prerogative is a part of the law, but 'Sovereign Power' is no parliamentary

[44] Quincy *Reports* (Mass.), 51–57 (1761), and Appendices at pp. 395–552, of which pp. 469–85 are especially relevant; also Adams, *Life and Works*, II, 521–25, and X, 232–362 *passim*.
[45] 2 Hansard, *Parliamentary History* (1628), 262–366.

word. In my opinion it weakens Magna Charta, and all the statutes; for they are absolute without any saving of 'Sovereign Power'; and should we now add it, we shall weaken the foundation law, and then the building must needs fall. Take heed what we yield unto: Magna Charta is such a fellow, that he will have no 'Sovereign.' " The words of Wentworth and Pym during the same debate were of like purport. Said the former, "These laws are not acquainted with 'Sovereign Power' "; to which Pym added that, far from being able to accord the king sovereign power, Parliament itself was "never possessed of it." Another noteworthy feature of the debate was the appearance in the course of it of the word "unconstitutional" in essentially its modern sense when used in political discussion.[46]

In his *Institutes* Coke, still the embattled commoner, completes his restoration of Magna Carta as the great muniment of English liberties. It is called "Magna Charta, not for the length or largeness of it . . . but . . . in respect of the great weightiness and weighty greatness of the matter contained in it; in a few words, being the fountain of all the fundamental laws of the realm." Declaratory of the common law, "this Statute of Magna Charta hath been confirmed above thirty times." Judgments and statutes against it "shall be void." Its benefits extend to all, even villeins, they being freemen as to all save their own lords. And what were these benefits? Especially they

---

[46] The occasion was Serjeant Ashley's expression of "divine right" sentiment. *Ibid.*, 317. "The doctrine advanced by this gentleman seemed so unconstitutional that he was ordered into custody." *Ibid.*, 328–29. George Chalmers in his *Political Annals* notes that the word "unconstitutional" was applied in New England to certain acts of Parliament in 1691. *New York Historical Society Collections* (1868), I, 81.

were the benefits of the historical procedure of the common law, the known processes of the ordinary courts, indictment by grand jury, trial by "law of the land," habeas corpus, security against monopoly, taxation by the consent of Parliament. Thus the vague concept of "common right and reason" is replaced with a "law fundamental" of definite content and traceable to one particular document of ancient and glorious origin.[47]

Coke's contribution to American constitutionalism is threefold: In the first place, his revival of Magna Carta is undoubtedly accountable in some indeterminate measure for the American idea that the constitution ought to be embodied in a fundamental *document*. In the second place, the influence of his sanctification of certain institutions and precedures of the common law, the grand jury, the petit jury, and the writ of habeas corpus especially, is evidenced to this day in the bills of rights of the national and State constitutions. In the third place, he clearly suggested judicial review of statutes, and judicial review of indefinite scope, although he may not have intended to ascribe to the ordinary courts the finality of decision which, thanks to Montesquieu and the principle of the separation of powers, America early came to do. The indispensability of the first two contributions to the final result is more or less speculative, that of the third is certain—as much so at least as such things can ever be said to be.

Let us at this point cast a brief backward glance over the argument thus far. We have been tracing the gradual contraction of the idea of *lex naturalis* conceived as the

[47] For this paragraph see 1 *Co. Inst.* 36 and 81; 2 *ibid.*, 45 and 57; and for a general commentary on Magna Carta, pp. 2–77.

informing principle of a universal moral order to a principle of limitation upon governmental action. Adopting the optimistic conception of human nature which was propagated by Stoicism, Cicero deduced from it the juristic notion of liberty in the sense of individual freedom of action; and this he found to be of two sorts, that which results from the restraints which authority imposes and that which the individual is entitled to claim as against authority when it lapses into injustice. Of these two conceptions only the latter was of much value to the early Middle Ages, which found in *immemorial custom* the principal reliance against the boisterous violence of military chieftains. And in medieval England the conception of a higher law delimiting authority attained a still stricter definition and corresponding solidity, being finally identified with certain principles and institutions of the common law, "to the cognizance of which long years of study were requisite." Natural law was contracted to the dimensions of a craft mystery.

Luckily for the survival of the idea of a law which derives its right to prevail from its own intrinsic qualities rather than its origination in this or that human will, the contracting process was at this moment arrested for the time being. For, as the quarrel between Parliament and the Stuarts passed from the stage of controversy to open warfare, it became evident, especially to the king's enemies, that some higher authority than that of the past must be invoked, first, because the system which had come down from the past was being shattered, and secondly, because it was necessary to address the nation at large in a language which could be understood by laymen as well as by lawyers. At this same period, Hugo

Grotius was endeavoring to resuscitate the Ciceronian conception of natural law in order to erect upon it a system of international law; and from Holland, which had become a refuge from Stuart wrath for English dissenters, the revived conception passed to England, whence in due course a particular version of it reached the American Colonies. I mean John Locke's second *Treatise on Civil Government* of 1691, which in justifying one revolution laid the ideological groundwork for another.[48]

The outstanding feature of Locke's treatment of natural law is the almost complete dissolution which this concept undergoes at his hands into the *natural rights* of the individual—the rights of "life, liberty, and estate." The dissolving agency by which he brings this transformation about is the doctrine of the Social Compact, with its corollary notion of the State of Nature. Men are by nature sociable and the state of nature was in the main an era of "peace, good will, mutual assistance and preservation," in which the "free, sovereign" individual was already in possession of "inalienable" rights of "life, liberty, and estate." The grand defect of the state of nature was its lack of "executive power," so that each man was compelled to defend his own against the casual, or deliberate trespasses of others. To remedy this shortcoming every man came in time to agree with his fellows to vest in the majority of them the right to create a government and endow it with coercive powers; thereby the state of nature made way for a *"civil"* or *"political"* society. Nevertheless, should the authority which was thus brought into being come at any time to be abused by its custodians persistently and of deliberation, their op-

[48] I am using Henry Morley's edition (1903).

pressed victims were entitled to overthrow them—to revert, in short, to the state of nature, and on this basis erect a new polity.[49]

While there are points of obvious difference between the Lockian system and its Ciceronian prototype which are of legitimate interest to the historian of political thought, these should not be permitted to obscure their points of agreement. These are, first, insistence upon the aptitude of men for social relations regardless of the institutions under which they live—the legacy of Stoicism; second, the dependence of political authority on the consent of the governed, an idea which is present in Cicero although it is not dramatized by him as it is by Locke; third, the idea, again explicit in Locke, implicit in Cicero, that certain human rights are anchored in a law which is of higher obligation than any that political authority can supply. All these are permanent elements of the tradition I am here endeavoring to trace.

The two features of the *Treatise* which have impressed themselves most definitely and immediately upon American constitutional law are the limitations which it lays down for legislative power and its emphasis on the property right broadly defined. The legislature is the supreme organ of Locke's commonwealth, and it is upon this supremacy that he depends in the main for the safeguarding of the rights of the individual. But for this very reason legislative supremacy is supremacy within the law, not a power above it.[50] In point of fact, the word "sovereign"

---

[49] John Locke, *Treatise on Civil Government*, see Chaps. II, III, VII, VIII (especially § 97), IX (especially § 124), XVIII and XIX (especially § 225).

[50] *Ibid.*, see Chap. XI, "Of the Extent of the Legislative Power."

is never used by Locke in its descriptive sense except in reference to the "free, sovereign" individual in the state of nature. In detail, the limitations which Locke specifies to legislative power are these: First, it is not arbitrary power. Not even the majority which determines the form of the government can vest its agent with arbitrary power, for the reason that the majority right itself originates in a delegation by free sovereign individuals who had "in the state of nature no arbitrary power over the life, liberty, or possessions" of others, or even over their own. In this caveat against "arbitrary power," Locke definitely anticipates the modern latitudinarian concept of "due process of law" as *reasonable law.*

"Secondly, the legislative . . . cannot assume to itself a power to rule by extemporary, arbitrary decrees, but is bound to dispense justice and decide the rights of the subject by promulgated standing laws, and known authorised judges." Nor may it vary the law in particular cases, but there must be "one rule for rich and poor, for the favorite at Court and the countryman at plough." In this pregnant passage, Locke foreshadows some of the most fundamental propositions of American constitutional law: *Law must be general; it must afford equal protection to all; it may not validly operate retrospectively; it must be enforced through courts; legislative power does not include judicial power.*

Thirdly, as also follows from its fiduciary character, the legislature "cannot transfer the power of making laws to any other hands: for it being but a delegated power from the people, they who have it cannot pass it over to others." More briefly, *legislative power cannot be delegated.*

Finally, *legislative power is not the ultimate power of the commonwealth,* for "the community perpetually retains a supreme power of saving themselves from the attempts and designs of anybody, even their legislators, whenever they shall be so foolish or so wicked as to lay and carry on designs against the liberties and properties of the subject." So while legislative supremacy is the normal sanction of the rights of men, it is not the final sanction. The identical power which was exerted against James II would in like case be equally available against Parliament itself.

Locke's bias in favor of property is best shown in the fifth chapter of the *Treatise,* where he brings the labor theory of value to the defense of inequality of possessions, and endeavors to show that the latter is harmonious with the social compact. His course of reasoning is as follows: All value, or almost all, is due to labor; and as there were different degrees of industry, so there were apt to be different degrees of possession. Yet most property, in those early days, was highly perishable, whence arose a natural limit to the accumulation of wealth, to wit, that no man must hoard up nature's bounty. Nevertheless, "the most exceeding of his just property," Locke is careful to insist, lay not "in the largeness of his possession, but the perishing of anything uselessly in it." Accordingly, when mankind, by affixing value to gold, silver, and other imperishable but intrinsically valueless things for which perishable commodities might be traded, made exchange possible, it thereby, as by deliberate consent, ratified unequal possessions; and the later social compact did not disturb this covenant.

So, having transmuted the law of nature into the rights

of men, Locke next converts these into the rights of ownership. The final result is to base his commonwealth upon the balanced and antithetical concepts of the rule of the majority and the security of property. But, thanks to "the labor theory of value," this is not the merely static conception that at first consideration it might seem to be. Taken up a century later by Adam Smith, the labor theory became the cornerstone of the doctrine of *laissez faire*. It thus assisted to adapt a political theory conceived in the interest of a quiescent landed aristocracy to the uses of an aggressive industrial plutocracy. At the same time, it also assisted to adapt a theory conceived for a wealthy and civilized community to the exactly opposed conditions of life in a new and undeveloped country. In a frontier society, engrossed in the conquest of nature and provided with but meager stimulation to artistic and intellectual achievement, the inevitable index of success was accumulation; and accumulation did, in fact, represent social service. The singular affinity, moreover, which Calvinistic New England early discovered for Lockian rationalism is in some measure explicable on like grounds. The central pillar of Calvinism was the doctrine of election. It goes without saying that all who professed this dogma believed themselves among the elect; yet of this what better, what more objective demonstration could there be than material success? Locke himself was a notable preacher of the gospel of industry and thrift.[51]

---

[51] See Chalfant Robinson, *Case of Louis The Eleventh and Other Essays* (1928); Max Weber, "Protestantische Ethick u. der 'Geist' des Kapitalismus," *Archiv Fur Sozial-Wissenschaft u. Sozial Politik*, XX (1904), 1–54, and XXI (1905), 1–110; Werner Sombart, *Quintessence*

Two other features of Locke's thought deserve brief comment. The first is his insistence upon the "public good" as the object of legislation and of governmental action in general. It should not be supposed that this in any way contradicts the main trend of his thought. Rather he is laying down yet another limitation on legislative freedom of action. That the public good might not always be compatible with the preservation of rights, and especially with the rights of property, apparently never occurs to him. A century later the possibility did occur to Adam Smith, and was waved aside by his "harmony of interests" theory.[52]

The scope which Locke assigns executive prerogative is, on the other hand, in view both of the immediate occasion for which he wrote and of his "constitutionalism," not a little astonishing. Of this he writes as follows: "Where the legislative and executive power are in distinct hands (as they are in all moderated monarchies and well-framed governments), there the good of the society requires, that several things should be left to the discretion of him that has the executive power: for the legislators not being able to foresee, and provide by laws, for all that may be useful to the community, the executor of the laws, having the power in his hands, has by the common law of nature a right to make use of it for the good of the society, in many cases, where the municipal law has given no direction, till the legislative can conveniently be as-

---

of Capitalism (1916), 257–62; and R. H. Tawney, "Puritanism and Capitalism," New Republic, XLVI (1926), 348.

[52] "Their [the legislature's] power, in the utmost bounds of it, is limited to the public good of the society." Locke, Treatise on Civil Government, Chap. XI, § 135; cf. §§ 89, 110, 134, 142, 158 with §§ 124, 131, 140.

sembled to provide for it; many things there are, which the law can by no means provide for; and those must necessarily be left to the discretion of him that has the executive power in his hands, to be ordered by him as the public good and advantage shall require: nay, it is fit that the laws themselves should in some cases give way to the executive power, or rather to the fundamental law of nature and government—viz., that as much as may be, all the members of the society are to be preserved." [53] Extrication from the trammels of a too-rigid constitutionalism through a broad view of "executive power" is a device by no means unknown to American constitutional law and theory.

Locke's contribution is best estimated in relation to Coke's. Locke's version of natural law not only rescues Coke's version of the English constitution from a localized patois, restating it in the universal tongue of the age, it also supplements it in important respects. Coke's endeavor was to put forward the historical *procedures* of the common law as a permanent restraint on power, and especially on the power of the English crown. Locke, in the limitations which he imposes on legislative power, is looking rather to the security of the *substantive* rights of the individual—those rights which are implied in the basic arrangements of society at all times and in all places. While Coke extricated the notion of fundamental law from what must sooner or later have proved a fatal nebulosity, he did so at the expense of archaism. Locke, on the other hand, in cutting loose in great measure from the historical method of reasoning, opened the way to the larger issues with which American constitutional law has been called

[53] *Ibid.*, Chap. XIV.

upon to grapple in its latest maturity. Without the Lockian or some similar background, judicial review must have atrophied by 1890 in the very field in which since that date it has been most active; nor is this to forget his emphasis on the property right. Locke's weakness is on the institutional side. While he contributed to the doctrinal justification of judicial review, it was without intention; nor does he reveal any perception of the importance of giving imperative written form to the constitutional principles which he formulates. The hard-fisted Coke, writing with a civil war ahead of instead of behind him, was more prescient.

Locke's is the last great name in the tradition of Liberty against Government that is common to our own country and England, and even in the *Treatise on Civil Government* a rift appears in the tradition which was destined to lead finally to the enthronement of judicial review in this country and that of the legal omnipotence of Parliament in Great Britain. The conception of a supreme legislature bound by higher law was too unstable to withstand long the fierce party contentions which succeeded the Glorious Revolution, and when the Whig Parliament in 1716 extended its own existence from three years to seven a precedent was created which could only be rationalized by appeal to the notion of a human lawmaking power uncontrolled by any existing law or institution.[54]

Even in the sixteenth century, as we saw earlier, Sir Thomas Smith had deduced from the ecclesiastical revolution of Henry VIII and his successors the notion of Parliament's legal omnipotence; and early in the seven-

[54] Albert Venn Dicey, *Introduction to the Study of the Law of the Constitution* (7th ed., 1908), 42–46.

teenth century the same conception was revived by James I's parliamentary foes as a means of subjecting the King-out-of-Parliament to the King-in-Parliament. Finally, in Thomas Hobbes's *Leviathan*, published forty years before Locke's second *Treatise*, the same idea was given a formulation which was designed in due time to put to rest permanently the idea of a law of transcendental obligation, and by so doing to establish the line between law and ethics.

Hobbes, who is said to have been a timid man, had been called upon to witness stern events, and his conception of the state of nature was dictated by these circumstances. In contrast with Locke's era of "peace, good will, and preservation," it is an era of "force and fraud," an era without arts, letters, or society, an era of "continued fear and danger of violent death, and the life of man solitary, poor, nasty, brutish, and short." Hobbes's conception of the purpose of the social compact is shaped in turn by his conception of the state of nature. Not until every individual has, by express agreement with every other, surrendered unconditionally and irretrievably his *natural* liberty to a sovereign prince or assembly capable of giving law to all, does *real* liberty, "the peace of the subjects within themselves and their defense against a common enemy," come into existence.[55]

The notion of rights anterior to the state thus goes a-glimmering. The only possible source of rights in any valuable sense is a *human sovereign-legislator;* their only possible definition is the like sovereign's commands— "*the civil law.*" The so-called "laws of nature" are in fact "not properly laws at all"; they are but "qualities that

[55] Thomas Hobbes, *Leviathan* (1651), Chaps. XIII, XVII, XVIII.

dispose men to peace and obedience." Only "when a commonwealth is settled, then are they actually laws . . . as being the commands of the commonwealth and therefore also civil laws." So while civil law and natural law may overlap as to content, it is not this which renders the former obligatory, but the fact that it is a command of "a sovereign prince or assembly." [56]

The apostle to America of the Hobbesian gospel of legislative sovereignty was Sir William Blackstone, of whose *Commentaries* nearly 2,500 copies had been sold on this side of the Atlantic prior to Lexington and Concord.[57] "Coke-Lyttleton, once the universal lawbook of students," was rapidly supplanted in the later days of the pre-Revolutionary controversy, and not at all to the advantage of the American cause, if we are to credit Jefferson's disparaging reference to that "brood of young lawyers" who, "seduced by the honeyed Mansfieldism of Blackstone, . . . began to slide into Toryism." [58] Nor, in fact, is Blackstone's appeal difficult to fathom. Eloquent, suave, as completely undismayed in the presence of palpable self-contradiction as "the Great Mr. Locke" himself, he is adept at insinuating new points of view without necessarily disturbing old ones—the very exemplar of legalistic and judicial obscurantism.

While still a student Blackstone had published an essay

---

[56] *Ibid.*, Chap. XXVI.

[57] The first volume appeared in 1765, the fourth in 1769. An American edition appeared in Philadelphia in 1771–72, of the full work, 1,400 copies having been ordered in advance. Charles Warren, *History of the American Bar* (1913), 178.

[58] Thomas Jefferson, *Writings* (Mem. Ed., 1903), XI, iv. Jefferson had no high opinion of "Blackstone lawyers." He termed them "ephemeral insects of the law."

on *The Absolute Rights of British Subjects*, and Chapter I of Book 1 of his greater work bears the same caption. Here he appears, at first glance, to underwrite the whole Lockian philosophy, but a closer examination discloses important differences. "Natural liberty" is defined as "the power of acting as one thinks fit, without any restraint or control, unless by the law of nature." It is "inherent in us by birth," and is that gift of God which corresponds with "the faculty of free will." Yet every man, Blackstone continues, "when he enters into society, gives up a part of his natural liberty as the price of so valuable a purchase," receiving in return "civil liberty," which is natural liberty "so far restrained by human laws (and no farther) as is necessary and expedient for the general advantage of the public." [59] The divergence between this and Locke's position is that while Locke also indicates public utility to be one requirement of allowable restraints upon liberty, it is by no means the sole requirement, nor invariably the ultimate one.

The divergence becomes even clearer when Blackstone turns to consider the positive basis of British liberties in Magna Carta and "the corroborating statutes." His language in this connection is especially complacent. The rights declared in these documents, he asserts, comprise nothing less than "either that residuum of natural liberty, which is not required by the laws of society to be sacrificed to public convenience, or else those civil privileges, which society hath engaged to provide in lieu of the natural liberties so given up by individuals. These, therefore, were formerly, either by inheritance or purchase, the rights

[59] I *Bl. Comm.* 125–26.

of all mankind; but, in most other countries of the world, being now more or less debased and destroyed, they at present may be said to remain, in a peculiar and emphatical manner, the rights of the people of England." [60] Nevertheless, when he comes to trace the limits of the "rights and liberties" so grandiloquently characterized, his invariable reference is simply to the state of the law in his own day.

So by phraseology drawn from Locke and Coke themselves, he paves the way to the entirely opposed position of Hobbes and Mansfield, whose defense of the Declaratory Act of 1766 was avowedly based on Hobbes. In elaboration of this position he lays down the following propositions: First, "there is and must be in all of them [states] a supreme, irresistible, absolute, uncontrolled authority . . ."; secondly, this authority is the "natural, inherent right that belongs to the sovereignty of the state . . . of making and enforcing laws"; thirdly, to the lawmaking power "all other powers of the state" must conform "in the execution of their several functions or else the Constitution is at an end"; and, finally, the lawmaking power in Great Britain is in Parliament, in which, therefore, the sovereignty resides. It follows, of course, that neither judicial disallowance of acts of Parliament nor yet the right of revolution has either legal or constitutional basis. To be sure, "acts of Parliament that are impossible to be performed are of no validity"; yet this is so only in a truistic sense, for "there is no court that has power to defeat the intent of the legislature, when couched in evident and express words." As to the right of revolution,

[60] *Ibid.*, 127-29.

"So long . . . as the English Constitution lasts, we may venture to affirm that the power of Parliament is absolute and without control." [61]

Nor does Blackstone in the end, despite his previous equivocations, flinch from the conclusion that the whole legal fabric of the realm was, by his view, at the Parliament's disposal. Thus he writes: "It hath sovereign and uncontrollable authority in the making, confirming, enlarging, restraining, abrogating, repealing, reviving, and expounding of laws . . . this being the place where that absolute, despotic power which must in all governments reside somewhere, is entrusted by the Constitution of these kingdoms. All mischiefs and grievances, operations and remedies that transcend the ordinary course of . . . the laws, are within the reach of this extraordinary tribunal. . . . It can, in short, do everything that is not naturally impossible, and therefore some have not scrupled to call its power by a figure rather too bold, the omnipotence of Parliament. True it is, that what the Parliament doth no authority upon earth can undo." [62] This absolute doctrine was summed up by De Lolme a little later in the oft-quoted aphorism that "Parliament can do anything except make a man a woman or a woman a man."

Thus was the notion of legislative sovereignty added to the stock of American political ideas. Its essential contradiction of the elements of theory which had been contributed by earlier thinkers is manifest. What Coke and Locke give us is, for the most part, cautions and safeguards against power; in Blackstone, as in Hobbes, we find the claims of power exalted. This occurred, moreover, at a moment when not merely the actual structure of govern-

[61] *Ibid.*, 49–51, 91, 161–62.   [62] *Ibid.*, 160–61.

ment in the United States, but a strong trend of thought among the American people afforded the thesis of legislative sovereignty every promise of easy lodgment. For, the Revolution, it must not be overlooked, was a contest for local autonomy fully as much as it was one for individual liberty, and the seat of local autonomy was the local legislative assembly. What more natural, then, than to conceive of the early State legislatures as counterparts of the British Parliament, accoutered with all the sovereign prerogatives of that body as it is depicted in the pages of Blackstone?

Why, then, did not legislative sovereignty finally engraft itself upon our constitutional system? The answer to this question brings us full circle back to the opening paragraph of this chapter. In the *written constitution* higher law finally achieved in this country a form which made possible the ascription to it of an entirely new kind of validity, the validity of a *statute emanating directly from the sovereign people*. For thus was the concept of *legislative* sovereignty, crowded to the wall by an enlarged, a revitalized conception of *popular* sovereignty. To Locke and his school, once government is set up, popular sovereignty is *functus officio* until the next revolution. The conception of popular sovereignty which underlies our written constitutions reaches back of Locke to the popular assemblies of ancient Greece and Rome. It is the conception which is invoked in the famous text of the *Institutes*, which I quoted at the outset of this chapter. The logical consequence of this development was the gradual absorption of higher-law concepts into the written constitution through the medium of judicial review. The subject is treated at length in the following pages.

CHAPTER III

LIBERTY INTO PROPERTY, BEFORE THE CIVIL WAR

IT IS axiomatic with most historians that the apparent similarity of today's institutions to those of the past should be approached, if not with suspicion, at least with circumspection. The relation of judicial review to the constitutional rights of the individual offers a case in point. Today the usual basis of judicial review in protection of such rights is the Bill of Rights, or equivalent provisions of the national and State constitutions. At the outset, however, the situation was markedly different.

Opinion was initially divided as to whether bills of right afforded a basis for judicial review at all. Madison, when it fell to his lot to pilot through the House of Representatives the proposals which eventually became the first ten amendments to the national Constitution, urged it as a point in their favor that they would implicate the judges in the defense of individual rights. "If," said he, "they are incorporated into the Constitution, independent tribunals of justice will consider themselves in a peculiar manner the guardians of those rights; they will be an impenetrable bulwark against every assumption of power in the Legislature or Executive; they will be naturally led to resist every encroachment upon rights expressly stipulated for in the Constitution by the declaration of rights." [1]

But in the *Federalist*, Madison's brother "Publius" had earlier made a very different assessment of bills of rights in general. Quoting in the eighty-fourth number of that publication the Preamble to the Constitution, he wrote: "Here is a better recognition of popular rights than volumes of those aphorisms which make the principal figure in several of our State bills of rights, and which would sound much better in a treatise of ethics." Yet in *Federalist*, 78, which is also from Hamilton's pen, is to be found the classic argument for judicial review, the principal source indeed of Marshall's historic opinion in Marbury *v.* Madison. And the latter's point of view was, in 1788, substantially the same as his mentor's. While asserting in the Virginia ratifying convention his belief that acts of Congress would be subject to judicial disallowance for unconstitutionality, he added the opinion that bills of rights were to be considered in relation to legislative power as "recommendatory" only. "Otherwise," said he, "many laws which are convenient would be unconstitutional." [2]

The main theme of this chapter, however, is the exact converse of the situation just discussed, and for it our point of departure is the case of Calder *v.* Bull,[3] which was decided by the Supreme Court in 1798. The immediate issue in the case was the validity of a special act of the Connecticut legislature which had upset a probate court decree with the ultimate result of bringing about its re-

[1] *Writings* (Hunt ed.), V, 385.
[2] Jonathan Elliot, *Debates* (1836), III, 509.   [3] 3 Dall. 386.

versal. Connecticut's constitution had at this date no bill
of rights, being still the royal charter of 1662, revamped
sufficiently to adapt it to the new status of national independence. Failing in consequence in their attack on the
legislative act under the local constitution, the defeated
parties appealed to the Supreme Court under the clause of
section 10 of Article I of the United States Constitution
which forbids the States to "pass ex post facto laws."
This time, too, they were disappointed. The Court, partly
in reliance on Blackstone and the *Federalist,* partly for
reasons of policy, construed the ban on ex post facto
laws as applicable to penal legislation only, but Justice
Samuel Chase incorporated in his opinion announcing this
result an apology which later citation of it has rendered
a landmark in the history of American constitutional
law.[4]

[4] The question of the merits of the Court's construction in Calder *v.*
Bull of the "ex post facto" clause is a little complicated. Professor W.
W. McCrosskey expresses the opinion in a recent article that the term
was intended to cover civil legislation made at the expense of vested
rights, and deduces a great amount of material more or less contemporary with the decision which tends to support this view. "The True
Meaning of the Constitutional Prohibition on Ex-Post-Facto Laws,"
14 *University of Chicago Law Review,* 539–64 (June, 1947). This also
is the view urged by William G. Hammond in his edition of Blackstone, in the following words: "The original meaning of *ex post facto*
applies to civil and criminal law alike. (Co. Litt. 241; Fearne's Con.
Rem. 175, 203; Powell on Devises, 113, 133, 134; 2 Raym. Ld. 1352.)
There are even some early American cases in which the same has been
held. (Den *v.* Goldtrop, Coxe, 272, 1 N.J.L. 1795; State *v.* Parkhurst,
4 Halst. 9 N.J.L. 427, 444, 1802.) No clearer example can be given of
Blackstone's controlling influence over the early law of the United
States, than the fact that this passage, which (as Judge Dixon has cor-
rectly said, 14 Vroom. 203; 39 Am. Rep. 558, 568) does not define the
term, but merely illustrates it from the criminal law, should have settled
the American sense of the term as relating only to penal or criminal

"I cannot subscribe," Chase declared, "to the *omnipotence* of a *state legislature*, or that it is *absolute* and *without control*, although its authority should not be *expressly* restrained by the *constitution or fundamental law* of the state. The people of the United States erected their constitutions . . . to establish justice, to promote the general welfare, to secure the blessings of liberty, and to protect persons and property from violence. The purposes for which men enter into society will determine the nature and terms of the social compact; and as they are the foundation of the legislative power, they will decide the proper objects of it. The *nature* and *ends* of *legislative* power will limit the *exercise* of it. . . . There are acts

law. It was from him no doubt that the limitation passed into the original constitution of Massachusetts (part 1, § 24); while in other states, still following him, the term 'retrospective laws' was used, but with limitations that confined it to criminal law, e.g., Maryland, art. 15; North Carolina, art. 24; Delaware, art. 11. But the application of the term was fully settled by the case of Calder *v.* Bull, 3 Dall. 386, 1798, in which it was held that a retrospective act, granting a new trial in a civil case, was not *ex post facto* within the meaning of the United States constitution." 1 *Comms.* (Hammond ed., 1890), 132. Earlier the same view was urged by Justice William Johnson in his opinion and accompanying note in 12 Wheat. 213 at 286 (1827), and in 2 Pet. 380 at 681–87 (1828). On the other hand, confusion as to the application of the "ex post facto" provision is to be found both in the Philadelphia Convention and in the State ratifying conventions. See Max Farrand (ed.), *Records of the Federal Convention*, II, 375–76, 439, 440, 448, 617, 636, 640; III, 165 and 328; also Elliot *Debates* (2d ed., 1861), II, 406–407; III, 472, 474, 476, 479; IV, 184–85. Undoubtedly the best argument for refusing to extend the "ex post facto" clause to civil legislation is the one stated by Iredell in note 6 *infra*. The same argument applied, although in less measure, to the Kentian taboo on "retrospective laws." (See pp. 74–75 *infra*.) It should be noted, too, that while the Kentian doctrine reached only State legislation, the constitutional prohibition of ex post facto laws reached national legislation as well. See Article I, § 9, cl. 3.

which the federal or state legislatures cannot do without exceeding their authority. . . . An *Act* of the legislature (for I cannot call it a *law*) contrary to the great principles of the social compact cannot be considered a rightful exercise of legislative authority. . . . A law that punishes an innocent action . . . ; a law that destroys, or impairs the lawful private contracts of citizens; a law that makes a man a judge in his own case; or a law that takes *property* from A and gives it to B; it is against all reason and justice for a people to entrust a legislature with *such* powers; and therefore it cannot be presumed that they have done it. The *genius*, the *nature*, and the *spirit* of our state governments amount to a prohibition of such acts of legislation; and the *general principles of law and reason* forbid them." [5]

To these views Chase's younger colleague Iredell demurred, being evidently of Jefferson's "brood of young lawyers" whose legal education had been based on Blackstone's *Commentaries*. "Some speculative jurists," Iredell conceded, had held "that a legislative act against natural justice must, in itself, be void," but the correct view was that if "a government composed of legislative, executive and judicial departments were established by a constitution which imposed no limits on the legislative power . . . whatever the legislative power chose to enact would be lawfully enacted, and the judicial power could never interpose to pronounce it void. . . . Sir William Blackstone, having put the strong case of an act of Parliament which should explicitly authorize a man to try his own cause, explicitly adds" that even in that case "there is no court that has the power to defeat the intent of the legisla-

[5] 3 Dall. 388–89.

ture" when couched in unmistakable terms. Besides, Iredell continued, "ideas of natural justice are regulated by no fixed standard: the ablest and purest men have differed upon the subject; and all that the court could properly say in such an event, would be that the legislature (possessed of an equal right of opinion) had passed an act which, in the opinion of the judges, was inconsistent with the abstract principles of justice." [6]

To which of these positions has history awarded the palm of victory? The answer to this question will be supplied in detail in the following pages. In general terms, it is that while Iredell's view has enjoyed in the final upshot a *formal* triumph, the *substance* of victory has gone to

[6] *Ibid.*, 398–99. Iredell continues: "The policy, the reason and humanity, of the prohibition, do not, I repeat, extend to civil cases that merely affect the private property of citizens. Some of the most necessary and important acts of Legislation are, on the contrary, founded upon the principle, that private rights must yield to public exigencies. Highways are run through private grounds. Fortifications, Lighthouses, and other public edifices, are necessarily sometimes built upon the soil owned by individuals. In such, and similar cases, if the owners should refuse voluntarily to accommodate the public, they must be constrained, as far as the public necessities require; and justice is done, by allowing them a reasonable equivalent. Without the possession of this power the operations of Government would often be obstructed, and society itself would be endangered. It is not sufficient to urge, that the power may be abused, for, such is the nature of all power,—such is the tendency of every human institution: and, it might as fairly be said, that the power of taxation, which is only circumscribed by the discretion of the Body, in which it is vested, ought not to be granted, because the Legislature, disregarding its true objects, might, for visionary and useless projects, impose a tax to the amount of nineteen shillings in the pound. We must be content to limit power where we can, and where we cannot, consistently with its use, we must be content to repose a salutary confidence. It is our consolation that there never existed a Government, in ancient or modern times, more free from danger in this respect, than the Governments of *America*."

Chase in what, on this very account, became in due course the most important field of American constitutional law.

As we saw in the preceding chapter, the American tradition of judicial review stems from Coke's dictum in Bonham's Case, and so antedates the earliest American constitutions by more than 160 years.[7] Nor has it ever ceased entirely to imbibe sustenance from its doctrinal source. A decade after Otis converted the dictum into a weapon against British pretensions in the Colonies, George Mason leveled it against an act of the Virginia colonial assembly under which certain Indian women had been sold into slavery. Said the future author of the Virginia Declaration of Rights: "If natural right, independence, defective representation, and disavowal of protection, are not sufficient to keep them from the coercion of our laws, on what other principles can we justify our opposition to some late acts of power exercised over us by the British legislature? Yet they only pretended to impose on us a paltry tax in money; we on our free neighbors, the yoke of perpetual slavery. Now all acts of the legislature apparently contrary to natural right and justice are, in our laws, and must be, in the nature of things, considered as void. The laws of Nature are the laws of God; whose authority can be superseded by no power on earth . . . all human constitutions which contradict their laws, we are in conscience bound to disobey. Such have been adjudications of our courts of justice." Mason concluded by citing Coke and his successor, Hobart. The court adjudged the act to have been repealed.[8]

Nor did either the achievement of independence or the

---

[7] See pp. 34–40 *supra*.
[8] Robin *v.* Hardaway, Jefferson, *Virginia Reports*, 109 (1772).

adoption of the Constitution consign the dictum to the scrap heap. In 1789 the Supreme Court of South Carolina ruled that when a literal reading of State legislative acts brought them into conflict with "the plain and obvious principles of common right and reason," the court must construe them in a way to avoid this result; and three years later the same court, growing bolder, declared an act of the Colonial assembly passed in 1712 to be absolutely void as against "common right and reason as well as Magna Carta." [9] The latter year too Justice Paterson of the new United States Supreme Court admonished a Pennsylvania jury that to construe a certain act of the State legislature in a way that would bring it into conflict with plaintiff's property rights would render it void. "The right of acquiring and possessing property, and having it protected," said he, "is one of the natural, inherent, and unalienable rights of man. Men have a sense of property. Property is necessary to their subsistence, and correspondent to their natural wants and desires; its security was one of the objects that induced them to unite in society. . . . The preservation of property . . . is a primary object of the social compact, and, by the late Con-

---

[9] Haws v. McClaws, 1 Bay (S.C.), 93 (1789); Bowman v. Middleton, *ibid.*, 252 (1792). Meantime, in Osborne v. Huger, the same court had declared that it would not construe a law so as to divest a right; that a retrospective law in that sense would be against the constitution of the State. *Ibid.*, 179. The first and third of these cases illustrate what may be termed "judicial review by construction." A still earlier example of the same thing is seen in the Symsbury case, which arose in Connecticut in 1784. Here a grant by the legislature in 1729, being found to overlap one made in 1670, was to that extent curtailed by the court. Kirby (Conn.), 444. All these cases are interesting also as showing the stimulation given to the establishment of judicial review by judicial concern for vested rights.

stitution of Pennsylvania, was made a fundamental law." [10]

The truth is that Iredell's tenet that courts were not to appeal to natural rights and the social compact as furnishing a basis for constitutional decisions was disregarded at one time or other by all of the leading judges and advocates of the initial period of our constitutional history, an era which closes about 1830. Marshall, it is true, had imbibed from Blackstone's pages much the same point of view as Iredell's. Yet on the crucial occasion of his decision in Fletcher v. Peck,[11] he openly appealed to "the nature of society and government" as setting "limits to the legislative power," and putting the significant query, "how far the power of giving the law may involve every other power," proceeded to answer it in a way that he could not possibly have done had he not, that once at least, abandoned Blackstone's guidance. The record of many others had not even this degree of ambiguity. Justices Chase, Paterson, Wilson, Chief Justices Grimke, Parsons, Parker, Hosmer, Ruffin, Buchanan all appealed on occasion to natural rights and the social compact as limiting legislative power, and based decisions on this ground, and the same doctrine was urged by the greatest lawyers of the period without reproach.[12]

[10] Vanhorne's Lessee v. Dorrance, 2 Dall. 304, at 310 (1792).

[11] 6 Cranch 87 (1810).

[12] Besides the cases already mentioned or to be mentioned *infra*, see the case Proprietors, etc. v. Laboree, 2 Greenl. (Me.), 275, 294 (1823); Emerick v. Harris, 1 Binn. (Pa.), 416 (1808); Whittington v. Polk, 1 Harr. & J. (Md.), 236 (1802); Jackson v. Catlin, 2 Johns. (N.Y.), 248 (1807); Stackpole v. Healy, 16 Mass. 33 (1819); Weister v. Hade, 15 Pa. St. 474 (1866), where copious citation of earlier State cases will be found.

How dominant were Justice Chase's "speculative" views with Bench and Bar throughout the period when the foundation precedents of constitutional interpretation were being established is well shown in the case of Wilkinson v. Leland,[13] decided by the Supreme Court in 1829. Attorney for defendants in error was Daniel Webster. "If," said he, "at this period, there is not a general restraint on legislatures, in favor of private rights, there is an end to private property. Though there may be no prohibition in the constitution, the legislature is restrained from acts subverting the great principles of republican liberty and of the social compact." To this contention his opponent William Wirt responded thus: "Who is the sovereign? Is it not the legislature of the state and are not its acts effectual, unless they come in contact with the great principles of the social compact?" The act of the Rhode Island legislature under review was upheld, but said Justice Story speaking for the Court: "That government can scarcely be deemed to be free when the rights of property are left solely dependent upon the will of a legislative body without any restraint. The fundamental maxims of a free government seem to require that the rights of personal liberty and private property should be held sacred."

Forty years later, however, Iredell appeared to have triumphed. In Cooley's *Constitutional Limitations*, first published in 1868, we read that courts may not set aside legislative acts on the ground of their violating "natural rights" and "the principles of republican government" unless these things have been stipulated for in the written

[13] 2 Pet. 627, at 646–47, 652, 657 (1829).

constitution.[14] But appearances are sometimes deceptive, and they were never more so than in this instance. For Cooley straightway adds: "It does not follow . . . that in every case the courts, before they can set aside a law as invalid, must be able to find some specific inhibition which has been disregarded." If no power has been granted to do a thing, then it is unnecessary to forbid its being done. To the legislature only *"legislative power"* has been granted, and what that term signifies is for the courts to say finally. In short, having ostentatiously expelled Chase's "speculative views" by the door, Cooley prepares a window for their readmission in different guise.[15]

Events were not slow in demonstrating that the early State constitutions, whether they were furnished with bills of rights or devoid of them, left one category of rights peculiarly exposed to legislative infringement—those which are associated with *ownership*. Everywhere legislative assemblies, energized by the reforming impulse of the period, were led to attempt results which, even when they lay within the proper field of lawmaking, we should today regard as requiring constitutional amendments to establish. Virginia, as Bancroft writes, used her "right of original and complete legislation to abolish the privileges of primogeniture, cut off entails, forbid the slave-trade, and establish the principle of freedom in religion as the inherent and inalienable possession of spiritual beings." Elsewhere the liberal forces of the hour assailed the vested interest of Negro slavery. Vermont, Massachusetts, and New Hampshire ridded themselves of slavery by con-

---

[14] Thomas M. Cooley, *Constitutional Limitations,* * 163–69. I am using the 1871 (2d) edition.
[15] *Ibid.,* 174–76, and citations.

stitutional amendment or in consequence of judicial construction of the constitution, while in Pennsylvania, Rhode Island, and Connecticut gradual emancipation was brought about by ordinary legislative enactment.[16]

Meantime, in the years following 1780 a general collapse in values had created for the time being a serious cleavage in American society between a debtor and a creditor class. The former comprised mainly farmers, who during the previous era of inflation had speculated in land freely. But though incapacitated financially, the farmers still controlled most of the State legislatures, which responded to their strident demands for relief with legislation that was highly destructive of credit values. The conclusion which the creditor class drew from these developments is recorded by Madison in *Federalist* No. 10. It was that when sharp divisions appear in society, republican institutions are not of themselves enough to guarantee the rights of the minority, or indeed "the permanent and aggregate interests of the community." And, he added, "those who hold and those who are without property have ever formed distinct interests in society." Indeed, there is no room for doubt that the anti-creditor activities of a majority of the State legislatures in the years preceding the Convention of 1787, climaxed as they were by Shays's rebellion in Massachusetts, where the legislature had held out against the demands of the debtor interest, had much to do with instigating the move-

[16] Edward S. Corwin, "The Progress of Constitutional Theory between the Declaration of Independence and the Meeting of the Philadelphia Convention," *American Historical Review*, XXX (1905), 511 ff.; George Bancroft, *History* (1892), V, 329; A. B. Hart, *Slavery and Abolition* (1906), 153; J. F. Jameson, *The American Revolution as a Social Movement* (Princeton Univ. Press, 1926). Cf. note 43 *infra*.

ment for constitutional reform which produced the Convention, and thereby the Constitution.[17]

The most persistent cause for discontent with the early State constitutions was, however, *internal* to those instruments and *functional*, the one indeed which received illustration in Calder *v.* Bull. Thanks to notions inherited from Colonial days, which were confirmed by the prevalent analogy between the State legislatures and the British Parliament, these bodies were prone during the early years of our constitutional history, and some of them for many years afterward, to all sorts of "special legislation" so called; enactments for revising or setting aside court decisions, for suspending the general law for the benefit of named individuals, for interpreting the law for particular cases, and even for deciding cases.[18] So long as there were Tories to attaint of treason this species of legislative activity was treated with complacence, but once this necessity was past such legislative practices fell rapidly into disrepute even with the stanchest friends of democracy.

A colloquy which arose early in the Philadelphia Convention as to that body's purposes points the moral. "The objects of the Union," Sherman of Connecticut declared, "were few," defense, domestic good order, treaties, the regulation of foreign commerce, revenue, to which Madison immediately rejoined: "He differed from the member from Connecticut in thinking the objects mentioned to be all the principal ones that required a National Gov-

[17] Andrew C. McLaughlin, *The Confederation and the Constitution* (1905), Chaps. IX and X.

[18] Article cited in note 16 *supra*, pp. 514–17; Edward S. Corwin, *Doctrine of Judicial Review* (Princeton Univ. Press, 1914), 69–71; 1 D. Chipman (Vt.), 22–24; Livingston *v.* Moore, 7 Pet. 469, 546–49 (1833); 13 *American Jurist* (1835), 72 ff.

ernment. Those were certainly important and necessary objects; but he combined with them the necessity, of providing more effectually for the security of private rights, and the steady dispensation of Justice. Interferences with these were evils which had more perhaps than anything else, produced this convention. Was it to be supposed that republican liberty could long exist under the abuses of it practiced in some of the States?" These views were heartily chorused by other members. The faulty organization of government within the States, threatening as it did, not alone the Union, but republican government itself, furnished the Convention with a problem of transcendent, even world-wide importance.[19]

The remedies which the Convention provided for these evils are set forth in the following words of section 10 of Article I of the Constitution: "No State shall . . . coin money; emit bills of credit; make any thing but gold and silver coin a tender in payment of debts; pass any bill of attainder, ex post facto law, or law impairing the obligation of contracts. . . ." So far as the interests of creditors are concerned these provisions have generally proved adequate as against State legislative power. But when we turn to "interferences with the steady dispensation of justice," the provision which was expected by many to remedy that evil was, as we have seen, to all intents and purposes struck from the Constitution in Calder *v.* Bull. The Justices, however, all except Iredell, regretted deeply the feeble course which the unpopularity of the federal judiciary at that date forced upon them, and Chase's dictum was undoubtedly intended as a challenge to the State judiciaries to fill the gap which the Court felt

19 Farrand (ed.), *Records,* I, 48, 133-34, 255, 424, 525, 533; II, 285.

it was creating in the Constitution. In the years following, these bodies responded valiantly.

We are thus brought to the genesis of what I have ventured to baptize *"the Doctrine of Vested Rights,"* the most prolific single source of constitutional limitations of any concept of American constitutional law.[20] The general purport of this doctrine was that *the effect of legislation on existing property rights was a primary test of its validity;* for if these were essentially impaired then some clear constitutional justification must be found for the legislation or it must succumb to judicial condemnation. Ultimately, as we shall see, the doctrine was brought within the four corners of the written constitutions of the several States, but at the outset its relation to these documents was external and peripheral. Indeed, most of the cases discussed or alluded to thus far in this chapter as illustrating judicial review on the basis of extraconstitutional principles also illustrate the doctrine of vested rights in its initial stages.

And it is partly owing to this circumstance that the doctrine revealed during this early period a capacity for growth which brought it into contact with other manifestations of legislative activity than the one which was most immediately responsible for its formulation. At the outset the doctrine was directed especially at legislation interfering with judicial decisions affecting vested rights. But soon the tenuous line separating such legislation from

[20] See note 9 *supra;* Cooley, *Constitutional Limitations,* Chap. XI; Charles R. Erdman, Jr., *The New Jersey Constitution of 1776* (Princeton Univ. Press, 1929), Chap. V; Edward S. Corwin, "Extension of Judicial Review in New York," 15 *Michigan Law Review* (1917); and cases cited *infra.*

enactments which altered the general law to the detriment of specified persons was passed, and the latter category too was brought to the test of the doctrine. Both these applications of the doctrine were tested, moreover, on the same double justification. Both classes of "special acts"— those interfering with the property rights of named parties prior to litigation, as well as those ensuing upon it —were, it was argued, "bills of pains and penalties"; were, indeed, to all intents and purposes ex post facto laws, even though not technically so. In short, *the punitive intention of all such measures was presumed and their justification from a public point of view foreclosed.*

To this line of reasoning, moreover, was soon brought the support of the principle of the separation of powers. That the "judicial power" was the power to decide cases was too clear for argument. But this meant, it was contended, that when the legislature interfered with a judicial decision, it was leaving its own sphere and invading that of the judiciary. Moreover, legislative power was characteristically the power to make "general laws," so that in enacting special laws of any kind, the legislature again abandoned its character and usurped the power which was especially adapted to determining the relation of individuals to the "standing law," namely, the judicial power.[21]

[21] See Merrill *v.* Sherburne, 1 N.H. 199, 204 (1819); Dash *v.* Vankleeck, 7 Johns. (N.Y.), 477 (1811); Ogden *v.* Blackledge, 2 Cranch 272 (1804); Cooley, *Constitutional Limitations*, citations in notes 14 and 15 *supra;* also pp. * 91–93 and * 169–73; and Sill *v.* Corning, 15 N.Y. 297, 303 (1857). Indeed, it is no exaggeration to say that the expulsion of State legislative power from the judicial field was the most important by-product of the effort of the State courts between 1800 and the Civil War to provide protection for property rights against that same power.

Finally, on the basis of English precedents, it was held "upon principle," to quote Justice Story, that "every statute," even one couched in general terms, "which takes away or impairs vested rights acquired under existing laws, or creates a new obligation, imposes a new duty, or attaches a new disability in respect to transactions or considerations already past, must be deemed retrospective," and for that reason void, since again it is the essential function of legislative power to provide for the future, while past transactions are the field of judicial competence.[22] The argument was supported by a maxim from Coke's *Institutes*, that "a legislative enactment ought to be prospective, not retrospective in its operation (*nova constitutio futuris formam imponere debit, non praeteritis*)"; but whereas the English courts had always treated this maxim as stating *a rule of statutory interpretation* which Parliament was admittedly able to circumvent by the use of sufficiently definite language, our courts under the leadership of Story and Kent came to treat it as a *rule of constitutional obligation* and as applying to unambiguous as well as ambiguous legislative provisions which affected proprietarian interests detrimentally. *Whatever the public policy underlying even general legislation, that policy*

And, naturally, these courts were not unaware that so long as the legislatures were permitted to revise judicial decisions judicial review as a whole rested on a very insecure foundation. See especially the discerning remarks of Justice Woodbury in Merrill *v.* Sherburne, cited above.

[22] Society *v.* Wheeler, 2 Gall. (U.S.C.C.), 105, 139 (1814); Fed. Cas. No. 13,156. For the maxim from Coke, see 2 *Inst.* 292. Cf. *Cod.* 1, 14, 7, which reads as follows: "*Leges et constitutiones futuris certum est dare formam negotiis, non ad facta praeterita revocari; nisi nominatim et de praeterito tempore et adhuc pendentibus negotiis cautum sit.*"

*must stop short of trespassing upon the rights of owner-
ship, at least "unduly" or "unreasonably."*
   In brief, *legislation must be general and prospective, and
its impact on the individual and his rights must be through
the medium of the courts.*
   Within two years of the utterance of the dictum in
Calder *v.* Bull we find the author of it asserting, "few of
the revolutionary acts would stand the rigorous test now
applied." The remark is strikingly confirmed in the case
of the Court of Appeals of Virginia, which between the
years 1797 and 1804 passed from giving, in the earlier
year, the most sweeping possible application to the law
forbidding entails to the verge of overturning the law
disposing of church lands, which was saved by the intervention of Providence; for had not a member of the
court died the night before the decision was to be rendered,
the court would have stood three to two against the act.[23]
   Another illustration of like import is the opinion of the
Supreme Judicial Court of Massachusetts in 1806 in the
case of Wales *v.* Stetson, which gives the doctrine of vested
rights the same effect as Marshall later gave the "obligation
of contracts" clause in the Dartmouth College case.
Eight years later the same court decided in Holden *v.*
James that notwithstanding the fact that the twentieth

   [23] Cf. Elliott *v.* Lyell, 3 Call (Va.), 268 (1802), which follows Lord
Mansfield's ruling in Couch *v.* Jeffries, 4 Burr. 2460 (1769); Carter *v.*
Tyler, 1 Call (Va.), 165 (1797); and Turpin *v.* Locket, 6 Call (Va.),
113 (1804). The legislation sustained in the last case was partially overturned by the United States Supreme Court in Terret *et al. v.* Taylor,
9 Cr. 43 (1815), a case coming up through the circuit. Justice Chase's
reference to "more rigorous tests" occurs in Cooper *v.* Telfair, 4 Dall.
14 (1800), the decision in which was sustained an Act of Attainder and
Confiscation passed by Georgia in 1782.

article of the State constitution contemplated a power inhering in the legislature to suspend the laws, such suspensions must be general, it being "manifestly contrary to the first principles of civil liberty, natural justice, and the spirit of our constitution and laws, that any one citizen should enjoy privileges and advantages which are denied to all others under like circumstances." [24]

This, to be sure, was to range somewhat beyond the precincts of the doctrine of vested rights; but five years later the New Hampshire Supreme Court in a case involving the doctrine in the strictest sense, placed it squarely on the theory of the separation of powers, which it interpreted as forbidding any and every interference by the legislature with judicial orders and decisions.[25] Meanwhile, in 1811, the principle of the prospective operation of statutes was annexed to the constitutional jurisprudence of New York by Chief Justice Kent in the once famous case of Dash v. Vankleeck.[26] Not content with Coke's endorsement of the rule, Kent purports to trace it, via Bracton, to Justinian's *Digest*, where the principle is stated "that the law-giver cannot change his mind to the prejudice of a vested right (*nemo potest mutare consilium suum in alterius injuriam*)." This principle, Kent asserts in the face of Blackstone's directly contrary language, limited even the omnipotence of Parliament.

It is Kent, indeed, who must be credited with giving the doctrine of vested rights its finally perfected and rounded form. This he was enabled to do in his *Com-*

[24] 2 Mass. 145; 11 *ibid.*, 396. With the former cf. 1 Yeates (Pa.), 260 (1793).   [25] Cited in note 21 *supra*.
[26] Cited in note 21 *supra*. See *Dig.* 17, 50, 75.

free state. Distinguishing these as the powers of *taxation*, *eminent domain*, and *regulation*, he then proceeded to "treat" each of them—in the chemical sense—in a sterilizing bath of vested rights. Taxation he held to be governed by the principle of *quid pro quo*, from which it followed that taxes must be "equal in proportion to the value of property," and, as his apostles later deduced, must be levied for "public purposes" only, inasmuch as it was only as a member of the public that the taxpayer could hope to receive his *quid pro quo*. The implication was, of course, that what was a "public purpose" was a question ultimately for the courts, doctrine which by 1880 had probably become accepted constitutional law in every State in the Union.[28]

In dealing with the power of eminent domain Kent was able to fall back upon a decision which he had rendered as Chancellor in 1816. This was in the leading case of Gardner *v*. Newburgh, in which the statute under review was one authorizing the trustees of the village of Newburgh to supply its inhabitants with water by means of conduits. While the statute made provision for the compensation of the owner through whose land the conduits were laid and of the owners of the springs from which the water was taken, it omitted to compensate Gardner through whose land the water had previously flowed. At this time there was no reference in the New York constitution to the eminent domain power. On the authority, however, of Grotius, Puffendorf, Bynkerschoeck, and Blackstone, Kent both asserts the existence of this power as an element of sovereignty and lays down the principles which limit it in favor of private property. The power

[28] 2 *Comms.* *332; Cooley, *Constitutional Limitations*, *487–95.

was exercisable "for necessary or useful *public* purposes"; indemnification was due not only for property taken but also for property damaged in consequence of the use that was made by the State of the property taken; nor was the legislature the final judge of "a full indemnification." A decade later Kent reaffirms these propositions in his *Commentaries;* and his exposition of them again makes it apparent that he regarded the requirement of a "public purpose" to be capable of judicial enforcement.[29]

The third power of government touching property rights, that of "regulation," Kent describes in these words: "But though property be thus protected, it is still to be understood, that the law-giver has a right to prescribe the mode and manner of using it, so far as may be necessary to prevent the abuse of the right to the injury or annoyance of others or of the public. The government may by general regulations interdict such uses of property as would create nuisances and become dangerous to the lives and health or peace or comfort of the citizens. Unwholesome trades, slaughter houses, operations offensive to the senses, the deposit of gunpowder, the building with combustible materials, and the burial of the dead, may all be interdicted by law, in the midst of dense masses of population, on the general and rational principle that every person ought so to use his property as not to injure his neighbors, and that private interests must be made subservient to the general interest of the community." [30] Likewise, he admits, there are "cases of urgent necessity" in which property may be destroyed, as when houses are razed to prevent the spread of a conflagration; but it is

[29] 2 Johns. Ch. 162 (1816); 2 *Comms.* *340 and notes.
[30] 2 *Comms.* *338 ff.

apparent from his citations that he regards the common law as making provision for such cases for the most part, and certainly has no intention of recognizing in the legislature an undefined power to create new types of nuisance or urgency. If, nevertheless, the legislature does this to the destruction of existing property values then it assumes the obligation to compensate owners even for "consequential or indirect" damage. The line, in Kent, between the regulatory power and the power of eminent domain is a wavering one.[31]

Even as Kent was bringing out his second volume, from which the above quotations are taken, a case was being decided in the New York courts which affords an instructive exemplification of his extremely moderate conception of the regulatory power of government in relation to the property right. This was the case of Vanderbilt *v.* Adams,[32] in which plaintiff in error contended that a statute authorizing harbor masters to regulate and station vessels in the East and North rivers did not extend to

[31] "It is admitted that even a statutory franchise, as a toll bridge or road, must yield to the sovereign right of eminent domain, and may be impaired or taken away, and appropriated to public uses whenever the public exigencies require it, for a franchise is fixed and determinate property; but it must be on the condition of making just compensation to the proprietors. Even if the damage be merely *consequential* or *indirect*, as by the creation of a new and rival franchise in a case required by public necessities, the same compensation is due, and the cases of Thurston *v.* Hancock, 12 *Mass. Rep.* 220, and Callender *v.* Marsh, 1 *Pick. Rep.* 418, are erroneous, so far as they contravene such a palpably, clear and just doctrine." 2 *Comms.* *339 note c, citing Gardner *v.* Newburgh and Story's opinion in Charles River Bridge *v.* Warren Bridge, 11 Pet. 638, 641 (1837). The decision in the latter case is discussed *infra.* For Kent's and Story's distress concerning it, see Charles Warren, *The Supreme Court in United States History* (1922), II, 302–305.
[32] 7 Cow. (N.Y.), 349 (1827).

owners of private wharves; or that if it did, it assumed to authorize an interference with private property that was beyond the constitutional powers of the State legislature. The argument was based on Gardner *v.* Newburgh, Dash *v.* Vankleeck, Fletcher *v.* Peck, and derivative cases. Although the court upheld the statute, it did so in markedly cautious language. Said Justice Woodworth: "It seems to me that the power exercised in this case is essentially necessary for the purpose of protecting the rights of all concerned. It is not in the legitimate sense of the term a violation of any right, but the exercise of a power indispensably necessary where an extensive commerce is carried on. . . . The right assumed under the law would not be upheld if exerted beyond what may be considered a necessary police regulation. The line between what would be a clear invasion of the right, on the one hand, and regulations not lessening the value of the right and calculated for the benefit of all must be distinctly marked. . . . Police regulations are legal and binding because for the general benefit and do not proceed to the length of impairing any right in the proper sense of the term. The sovereign power in a community, therefore, may and ought to prescribe the manner of exercising individual rights over property. It is for the better protection and enjoyment of that absolute dominion which the individual claims. . . ."

In short, the regulatory power existed primarily for the benefit of property itself—a doctrine which later courts professed to find embodied in Coke's maxim of *"sic utere ut alienum non laedas* (so use your own that you do not injure another man's property)," or in broader terms, "so that you do not injure another man's rights." [33]

Lastly, the doctrine of vested rights was infused by the Supreme Court of the United States into the "obligation of contracts" clause of the federal Constitution. The medium by which the doctrine was conveyed to this use was furnished by the circuit courts, which in cases falling to the jurisdiction of the national judiciary because of diversity of citizenship stand in the place of the State courts and so had, from the outset, felt free to pass upon the constitutionality of State laws under the State constitution and such "general principles" as they found those constitutions to recognize. This is the explanation of such decisions as that of Justice Paterson in Vanhorne *v.* Dorrance, mentioned earlier, of Story in Society *v.* Wheeler, and of the Supreme Court itself, speaking through Story, in Terret *v.* Taylor.[34] But the benefits of such decisions were, after all, not widespread. It was necessary if the doctrine of vested rights was to do its full work that it should enter the States themselves, and its protection through the federal judiciary be extended to legislative grants, whether of lands or charters, which, even in the States whose courts generally enforced the doctrine of vested rights, were sometimes left to the mercy of legislative majorities, in the thought apparently that what the legislature had given the legislature was entitled to take away. In Fletcher *v.* Peck, a case coming up from the circuit, Chief Justice Marshall achieves the deftest kind of blending of the doctrine of vested rights with the pro-

---

[33] The maxim occurs in 9 Rep. 57, 59 (1611), where it is treated as a rule only of private conduct. See Broom, *Legal Maxims* (8th Am. ed., 1882), *365 ff.   [34] See *ante* notes 10, 22, and 23.

hibition of the national Constitution of State laws impairing the obligation of contracts. In the Dartmouth College case, which came up on a writ of error from a State supreme court, the same doctrine was reiterated. The step was an easy one, and it was assisted by Webster's argument, a considerable part of which simply reproduced Jeremiah Mason's earlier argument before the State court invoking the doctrine of vested rights.[35]

A decade later, in 1829, Justice Johnson made an interesting confession of the motives that had guided the Court in this most important class of decisions: "This court," he wrote, "has had more than once to toil up hill in order to bring within the restriction of the states to pass laws violating the obligation of contracts, the most obvious cases to which the Constitution was intended to extend its protection; a difficulty which it is obvious might often be avoided by giving to the phrase *ex post facto* its original and natural application." [36] Although the suggestion of Justice Johnson fell upon stony ground, it would be easy today to imagine that the Supreme Court, in the interpretation that it began giving the "due process of law" clause of the Fourteenth Amendment about 1890, had heard and heeded the warning of sixty years before.

The doctrine of vested rights in the various embodiments which have been described above attained its maturity and its greatest reach of influence about 1830. Meanwhile, forces destined to bring about the doctrine's transference to a new basis in the State *written* constitu-

---

[35] 6 Cranch 87 (1810); 4 Wheat. 518 (1819).

[36] Note appended to his opinion in Satterlee *v.* Matthewson, 2 Pet. 380, 681 ff. (1829).

tion, where by Iredell's thesis it had to be if it was to be at all, had been gradually recruiting strength. Spearheading these was the doctrine of popular sovereignty. As exemplified in the Constitution of the United States, this doctrine ascribed to the people at large a *lawmaking* capacity paramount to that of their legislative representatives; and in the years following the adoption of the Constitution this conception of popular sovereignty enjoyed steady reinforcement from the appearance in an increasing number of States of the *constitutional convention* as part and parcel of the regular institutional setup. And in more palpable and concrete ways, too, the idea of popular sovereignty threatened the security of the doctrine of vested rights. In stimulating the cause of manhood suffrage it aided in the creation of a new electorate, and thus in exciting new popular expectations which could only be realized through the State legislature. Free schools, canals, railroads were among such expectations. In the final upshot, it is true, the demand for canals and railroads was, in consequence of the financial collapse of 1837, met by private companies, endowed, nevertheless, with the power of eminent domain, and requiring first and last a good deal of legislative regulation. The new electorate was, moreover, highly susceptible to appeals of a moral nature, to crusades against the legal disabilities of women, slavery, and intoxicants; and in each instance the legislation demanded in the name of reform was calculated to exact a heavy toll of vested interests.[37]

The rising argument for legislative power also drew

[37] The property right itself came under direct attack during this period, although such views seem to have been sporadic. See Arthur M. Schlesinger, Jr., *The Age of Jackson* (1945), 299–304.

sustenance at times from outside sources. In Coates v. Mayor,[38] a New York case which was decided in the same year as Vanderbilt v. Adams but by a different court, the statute under review authorized New York City to make by-laws "for regulating, or if they found it necessary, preventing the interment of the dead" within the city, and in pursuance of this statute the city had passed a prohibitory ordinance which plaintiffs in error claimed invaded their vested rights. "The legislature," said they, "cannot take away a single attribute of private property without remuneration"—a proposition which they supported by appropriate references to Kent, Gardner v. Newburgh, Fletcher v. Peck, and so on. To meet this attack the attorneys for the city were forced to levy upon doctrine from an alien jurisdiction—none other in fact than the Supreme Court of the United States. Thus in Gibbons v. Ogden, Chief Justice Marshall had described the field of legislation left to the States by the Constitution of the United States in very broad terms, and this description was now utilized to show the scope of legislative power under the State constitution in relation to the property right. Again, in McCulloch v. Maryland, Marshall had construed the words "necessary and proper" of the United States Constitution as meaning "expedient," and it was now urged that the term "necessary" in the legislative grant of power to the municipality must be similarly defined. Then, in Martin v. Mott, the Supreme Court had ruled that where a discretionary authority was vested by the Constitution in the President, its use was not subject to judicial review. The same line of argument was now contended to be applicable to a State legislature in the

[38] 7 Cow. (N.Y.), 585 (1827).

exercise of its powers. "The power in question," declared defendant's attorney, "is a legislative power, which must, on the subject of regulation, be transcendent. The legislators are the judges and their decision must be conclusive. Even a general law to prevent the growing of grain throughout the state, however despotic, could not be disobeyed as wanting constitutional validity." [39]

The by-law and the statute upon which it was based were both sustained. Speaking to the question of the necessity of the former, the court said: "This necessity is not absolute. It is nearly synonymous with expediency or what is necessary for the public good." To judge of that matter is the function of the legislature, it being "of the nature of legislative bodies to judge of the exigency upon which their laws are founded." And the law itself is "equivalent to an averment that the exigency has arisen, been adjudicated and acted upon." The duty of the court is merely to see "that the law operates upon the subject of the power."

Ten years later the Supreme Court under the presidency of Chief Justice Taney made a far more important contribution to the enlargement of views regarding State legislative power. This was in the celebrated case of the Charles River Bridge Co. *v.* the Warren Bridge Co., in which the question at issue was whether the former company's charter impliedly endowed it with a monopoly of the right to furnish transportation across the Charles River for an unstipulated distance. The new Jacksonian States'-rights Supreme Court answered this question in the negative, holding that "in a public grant nothing passes

[39] Citing 9 Wheat. 1 (1824); 4 Wheat. 316 (1819); 12 Wheat. 19 (1827).

by implication." "The object and end of all government," said Chief Justice Taney, "is to promote the happiness and prosperity of the community by which it is established; and it can never be assumed, that the government intended to diminish its power of accomplishing the end for which it was created. . . . While the rights of private property are sacredly guarded, we must not forget that the community also have rights, and that the happiness and well-being of every citizen depends on their faithful preservation." [40]

In these words Kent's "power of regulation," much to its author's dismay, be it said, took on new dimensions; became, in a word, "the Police Power" of American constitutional law. What the appearance of this vastly important rubric signified was this: *that legislation affecting vested rights detrimentally must nevertheless be judged from the point of view of the assumption that the legislature intended thereby to promote the public interest, not to punish the holders of the said vested rights;* and that in the absence of specific constitutional provision to the contrary the public interest was ordinarily entitled to prevail against such vested rights.[41]

[40] 11 Pet. 420, 547–48, 552 (1837).

[41] Quite liberal views regarding State legislative power sometimes crop up in unexpected places. See, e.g., Attorney General *v.* Stevens, N.J. Eq. 369 (1813), where the social compact is invoked as the basis of the rights of the community; and Scudder *v.* Trenton and Delaware Falls Co., 1 N.J. Eq. 696 (1832). Conversely, the doctrine of vested rights was sometimes disparaged, even in conservative New York: "Vested rights are indefinite terms, and of extensive signification; not infrequently resorted to when no better argument exists, in cases neither within the reason or spirit of the principle. Government was instituted for the purpose of modifying and regulating these rights with a view to the general good; and under the constitution the mode

Furthermore, the Court gave unambiguous notice in its opinion in the Charles River Bridge case that aside from the "obligation of contracts" clause the Constitution of the United States contained no provision protective of vested rights as against State legislative power.[42] Thus it *became more and more evident that the doctrine of vested rights must, to survive, find anchorage in some clause or other of the various State constitutions.* As it chanced, one such clause had already, prior to 1837, been put forward tentatively in the North Carolina jurisdiction with this very end in view, the "law of the land" clause of that State's constitution; and the historic counterpart of this clause, the "due process of law" clause which made its debut in American constitutional usage in the national Bill of Rights in 1791, was presently to be nominated for a similar role in the influential New York jurisdiction. Both clauses possessed the advantage that the precise historical significance of the terms "law of the land" and "due process of law" was shrouded in considerable mystery, but the "due process" clause finally

---

by which it was thought this object might best be attained, was left to the wisdom and discretion of the people themselves." Justice Nelson in People *v.* Morris, 13 Wend. (N.Y.), 329 (1835). See also Watson *v.* Mercer, 1 Watts (Pa.), 331 (1833); and Menges *v.* Wertman, 1 Pa. St. 218 (1845). The concept of State Sovereignty was yet another source from which the rising doctrine of the police power recruited strength. See especially Justice Barbour's opinion in City of New York *v.* Miln, 11 Pet. 102, 139; Chief Justice Taney's opinion in the License Cases, 5 How. 504, 583 (1847); and Justice Daniel's opinion in West River Bridge Co. *v.* Dix, 6 How. 507 (1848). In the first two of these cases the Court was concerned with the relation of the "commerce" clause to State legislative power. And see generally W. G. Hastings in *Proceedings of the American Philosophical Society,* XXXIX (1900), 359 ff.; also note 66 *infra* and note 47, Chapter IV.

[42] 11 Pet. at 539–40.

won out because it also contained the words, at once comprehensive and compendious, "liberty" and "property." [43]

The "law of the land" clause of the early State constitutions was usually a nearly literal translation of the famous chapter 29 of the Magna Carta of 1225, the Magna Charta of history. [44] The rendition of it in the Massachu-

---

[43] It is a curious fact that the right to trial by jury was first invoked for the purpose later served by the "law of the land" and "due process" clauses. When a considerable movement developed in New Jersey for a manumission of slaves by act of the legislature, the objection was raised that any member of that body voting for such a measure would violate his oath to preserve trial by jury. "Our most excellent constitution admits not the subject to be deprived of his life, liberty or property, but by a trial by a jury of his equals; and lest this inestimable privilege, the glory of freemen, should be infringed on, the constitution expressly requires that no member of the legislature shall possess a seat in the House, until he has solemnly sworn that he will maintain this immunity inviolate. It becomes, therefore, one of the unalterable particulars of our rights, and cannot be relinquished by the guardians of our liberties but at the expense of perfidy, and even of perjury itself. The liberation of our slaves, therefore, without the concurrence of their possessors, we apprehend, is an object infinitely further distant from the legal attention of our assembly, than are the heavens above the earth." Frank Moore, *Diary of the American Revolution* (1859), II, 362 (under date of January 1, 1781). We have also the following notes of a speech by Madison in the Virginia House of Delegates in November, 1786, against a bill to authorize an emission of paper money: "*Unconstitutional* 1. Affects rights of property as much as taking away equal value in land; illustrated by case of land paid for down and to be conveyed in future, and of a law permitting conveyance to be satisfied by conveying a part only—or other land of inferior quality—2. affects property without trial by Jury." *Writings* (Hunt ed., 1901), II, 280. It is interesting to compare this argument with that of Chief Justice Chase in Hepburn *v.* Griswold, in which in 1869 the Civil War Legal Tender Act was held void as, among other objectionable things, transgressing the "due process" clause of Amendment V. 8 Wall. 603, 624.

[44] The Latin is quoted in note 25, Chapter II, *supra*.

setts constitution of 1780 still reads: "No subject shall be arrested, imprisoned, despoiled, or deprived of his property, immunities, or privileges, put out of the protection of the law, exiled, or deprived of his life, liberty, or estate, but by the judgment of his peers or the law of the land." The phrase "due process of law" comes from chapter 3 of the statute 28 Edward III (1355) which reads as follows: "No man of what state or condition he be, shall be put out of his lands or tenements, nor taken, nor imprisoned, nor disinherited, nor put to death, without he be brought to answer by due process of law."

In his *Institutes* Coke asserts the complete identity in meaning of the two expressions, which he explains as signifying "due process of the common law," that is, "indictment or presentment of good and lawful men . . . or . . . writ original of the common law." Both phrases, in short, were intended to consecrate certain methods of trial; and neither bore any reference to those principles of "common right and reason" which Coke had invoked in Dr. Bonham's Case.[45]

Of the two earliest reported State cases involving the "law of the land" clause, both arose in 1794, one in North Carolina, the other in South Carolina. In the former "law of the land" was interpreted as signifying simply "a law for the people of North Carolina, made or adopted by themselves by the intervention of their own legislature." In the South Carolina case, on the other hand, the equivalent clause in that State's constitution was held to signify trial by jury in serious cases, and on this ground a legislative enactment which permitted a municipal court, pro-

---

[45] 2 *Inst.*, 50–51. See also Appendix to the present work.

ceeding without a jury, to levy a fine of £100, was held void.[46]

The initial effort to throw the "law of the land" clause about the doctrine of vested rights came from North Carolina also some ten years later. This occurred in the case of the University of North Carolina *v.* Foy.[47] The constitutional issue was created by a legislative act which repealed an earlier grant of lands to the University. Although the case is an exact parallel of the later case of Fletcher *v.* Peck, nobody seems to have supposed that the "obligation of contracts" clause was pertinent to its solution. The act was nevertheless held void under the "law of the land" clause of the State constitution. As the court put the matter: "The property vested in the trustees must remain . . . for the uses intended for the university, until the judiciary of the country in the usual and common form pronounce them guilty of such acts as will in law amount to a forfeiture of their rights. . . ."

[46] ——— *v.* State, 2 Hayw. (N.C.), 29, 38; Zylstra *v.* Charleston, 1 Bay (S.C.), 384. Plaintiff in the latter case had been arrested for violating a city ordinance which forbade the keeping of a tallow-chandler's shop within the corporation limits. It should be observed that his objections were leveled not at all against the substance of the ordinance in question, that is, the prohibition enacted by it of the further pursuit of his livelihood within the city limits, but solely against the manner in which that prohibition was enforced. A classic instance of the use of "due process of law" in the adjective sense, that is, as limiting the legislative power in the devising of procedure, is furnished by Justice Curtis' opinion in Murray *v.* Hoboken Land Co. 18 Howard 272 (1855): "The words due process of law were undoubtedly intended to convey the same meaning as the words 'by the law of the land' in Magna Carta. . . . The article is a restraint on the legislature as well as on the executive and judicial powers of the government, and cannot be so construed as to leave Congress free to make any process 'due process of law' by its mere will."   [47] 2 Hayw. (N.C.), 310 (1804).

In these words we encounter at the outset the abiding characteristic of all appeals to the "law of the land" or "due process" clauses for the purpose of incorporating the doctrine of vested rights into the written constitution. This is the assumption, *carried over from the doctrine itself*, that when anybody is deprived of his conceded property rights, except by the power of eminent domain, it is with a view to *punishing* him, which can be done only by judicial—i.e., "due"—process; and *of course the courts can enforce only the standing law, in other words, the law as it stood before the penalizing statute was enacted.*[48]

University of North Carolina *v.* Foy is susceptible of two interpretations, a narrow one and a broad one. On the one hand emphasis may be laid upon the special character of the enactment overthrown and the decision classified accordingly with those reviewed above, in which the judges were endeavoring to rid legislative power of its element of parliamentary prerogative by emphasizing the general character of legislation. This is the interpretation which Webster made of the case in his argument in Dartmouth College *v.* Woodward, where he defined "law of the land" to mean the "general law," and prohibitive therefore of "acts of attainder, bills of pains and penalties . . . legislative judgments, degrees, and forfeitures." A decade later Webster's language was in turn invoked by the Supreme Court of Tennessee in a case in which the "law of the land" clause of that State's constitution was construed to mean "a general public law equally binding upon every member of the community . . . under sim-

---

[48] It will be observed again how the principle of the separation of powers helps out this argument. See also notes 21 *supra* and 63 *infra*.

ilar circumstances." In 1832, like doctrine was voiced by the Supreme Court of South Carolina, and in 1838 by the Supreme Court of Maryland. And, in 1843, Chief Justice Gibson of Pennsylvania, earlier an avowed sceptic of both judicial review and the doctrine of vested rights, was driven in order to avoid too outrageous consequences from a "special act," to avail himself, at least *ad hoc*, of the definition of "law of the land" as "a pre-existent rule of conduct." [49] Indeed, it may be asserted with fair accuracy that by 1860 application of the "law of the land" clause as signifying "a general rule" had been pretty generally accepted throughout the country.

The broad interpretation of University of North Carolina *v.* Foy is to be arrived at by disregarding the special character of the act under review and treating the doctrine of that decision as translating the "law of the land" provision into a prohibition of *all* retrospective legislation whether general or special; and in the case of Hoke *v.* Henderson,[50] decided in 1833, the Supreme Court of North Carolina itself gave its precedent exactly this interpretation. In that case the statute involved, in providing for the future election of court clerks, operated when given a literal interpretation to displace previous incumbents by appointment. In behalf of the statute it was urged, first, that it was general in terms, "wanting in the precision and direct operation usually belonging to and distinguishing judicial proceedings," and, secondly, that it was—ostensibly at least—enacted from the standpoint

---

[49] 4 Wheat. at 575–82 (1819); Van Zant *v.* Waddell, 2 Yerg. (Tenn.), 260 (1829); State *v.* Hayward, 3 Rich. (S.C.), 389, (1832); 9 Gill & J. (Md.), 362 (1838); Norman *v.* Heist, 6 W. and S. (Pa.), 171 (1843).
[50] 2 Dev. (N.C.), 1.

of the legislative view of the public interest and without any intention of passing sentence upon those detrimentally affected by it, who in fact were not charged with any delinquency. The measure therefore was not, it was insisted, a bill of pains and penalties, and any discussion of procedure was impertinent to the issue.

Chief Justice Ruffin, unmoved by these arguments, proceeded to define "law of the land" to require that, before anyone shall be deprived of property, he shall have a judicial trial "according to the mode and usages of the common law" "and a decision upon the matter of rights as determined by the law under which it [the property] vested." Thus, *with reference to any particular property right, the existent law is elevated to the position of a constitutional limitation upon the legislative power and so can never be altered to the diminution of that right.* To be sure, the Chief Justice added, "the whole community may modify the rights which persons can have in things or at its pleasure abolish them altogether," but the community spoke only through the constitution.[51]

[51] Some five years after Hoke *v.* Henderson the case of *Ex parte Dorsey*, 7 Porter (Ala.), 293, arose under article I, section 10 of the Alabama constitution of 1819. Here the term "due course of law," from 25 Edw. III, is used in lieu of "law of the land." The case is further notable because in the controlling opinion by Judge Ormond the term "property" in the "due course of law" provision takes on a greatly expanded significance, connoting not merely, as did the phrase "vested rights," tangible property or specific franchises or remedies, but the general rights of an individual as a member of the community. Justice Collier dissented, upon the ground that the State constitution was not a grant of powers but an organization of inherent powers, which were accordingly available to the legislature unless specifically withheld. The "due course of law" clause had therefore no independent force as a limitation upon the power of the legislature. It meant such "forms of arrest, trial, and punishment" as were "guarantied by the Constitution,

It was not destined, however, that the doctrine of due process of law should enter the general constitutional jurisprudence of the United States through the Supreme Court of North Carolina. Some court more generally eminent in the world of citation and precedent was demanded for the business, and the jurisdiction that best met this requirement was the one in which the great Kent had lived and wrought.[52] At the same time, the situation confronting the New York courts from about 1830 on

---

or provided by the common law, or else such as the legislature, in obedience to constitutional authority, have enacted to insure public peace or elevate public morals." Two years later we find Justice Ormond substantially disavowing his doctrine in this case and adopting that of his dissenting associate. This was in the case of Mobile v. Yuille, 3 Ala. 137 (1841), in which the question was the power of the legislature to authorize a municipality to regulate the weight and price of bread. The attorney for defendant in error "strenuously contended," on the basis of Ormond's opinion in the Dorsey case, "that no such power exists because it would interfere with the right of a citizen to pursue his lawful trade or calling in the mode his judgment might dictate." But, rejoined Justice Ormond, "The legislature having full power to pass such laws as is [sic] deemed necessary for the public good, their acts cannot be impeached on the ground that they are unwise or not in accordance with just and enlightened views of political economy, as understood at the present day . . . arguments against their policy must be addressed to the legislative departments of government." See also State v. Maxey, 1 McMul. (S.C.), 501 (1837).

[52] Indeed, Kent himself had invoked, somewhat fleetingly, the "law of the land" clause in Gardner v. Newburgh, probably in reliance on University v. Foy. See 2 Johns. Ch. at 168. Years earlier Kent had, as a member of the New York Council of Revision, opposed a bill altering the charter of New York City, on the ground that "it has been considered as a settled and salutary principle in our government that, in all cases where the ordinary process of law affords a competent remedy, charters of incorporation containing grants of personal and municipal privileges were not to be essentially affected without the consent of the parties concerned." John M. Shirley, *The Dartmouth College Causes* (1879), 254.

caused them to turn with increasing eagerness to North Carolina's solution of the problem of reconciling an adequate supervision over legislative power with due deference to the now burgeoning principle of popular sovereignty.

Of the three powers of government recognized by Kent the one which at this period was most in the public eye was the power of eminent domain. Within a few years hundreds of canal and railroad companies were chartered by New York and endowed with power to condemn private property for rights of way. Yet could it be contended that employment by a private corporation of the power of eminent domain primarily in its own interest was for a "public purpose"? Ultimately the New York courts answered "yes"; the State function of providing public highways did not cease being a State function merely because the State chose to discharge it through the agency of private companies.[53] The strain put on Kent's doctrine by this logic was nevertheless still considerable, and when the legislature began endowing individuals with the right to condemn their neighbors' land for private highways, it became evident that the Kentian doctrine must either be brought within the written constitution or discarded.

The leading case in this context is Taylor v. Porter,[54] in which in 1843 just such a legislative act was held to

[53] Beekman v. Saratoga, etc. R.R., 3 Paige (N.Y.), 45 (1831); Bloodgood v. Mohawk, etc. R.R., 18 Wend. (N.Y.), 1 (1837).

[54] 4 Hill (N.Y.), 140; preceded by the Matter of John and Cherry Sts., 19 Wend. (N.Y.), 676. In Pennsylvania the right of the State to employ the power of eminent domain for the purpose of laying out private roads was contemporaneously sustained. Pacopson Rd. Case, 16 Pa. St. 15 (1851).

violate both the "law of the land" clause of the State constitution and the more recently added "due process of law" clause. Justice Bronson based his argument for the court on the decision in Hoke *v.* Henderson, a holding recommended by Kent at the time of its rendition as "replete with sound constitutional doctrine." So on the authority of Chief Justice Ruffin's opinion in the North Carolina case, "law of the land" is asserted to mean that before a man can be deprived of his property "it must be ascertained judicially that he has forfeited his privileges, or that someone else has a superior title to the property he possesses." But, if there was doubt as to the meaning of the phrase "law of the land," at least there could be none as to that of "due process of law," which meant nothing "less than a proceeding or suit instituted and conducted according to prescribed forms and solemnities for ascertaining guilt or determining the title to property." One exception to this definition was indeed furnished by an exercise of the power of eminent domain, when due process of law meant "due compensation"; but that power could be exercised for a public purpose *only.* Who then was to ascertain whether a given purpose was a public one if not the courts, as preliminary to their task of determining whether due process of law had been observed? Justice Nelson accepted "the general principle" of the decision, but confessed himself uncertain as to the grounds it rested on.

In Taylor *v.* Porter we again encounter the fundamental assumption underlying the doctrine of vested rights, *the assumption that any legislation impairing such rights was punitive in intention, a bill of pains and penalties, inherently beyond legislative power.* In Holmes *v.*

Holmes, decided in 1847, the recently enacted Married Women's Property Act, although a general law, was brought to the test of the same assumption and pronounced void under the "obligation of contracts" clause of the federal Constitution, a result which was referred in White *v.* White two years later to the doctrine of natural rights and, on the authority of Taylor *v.* Porter, to the "due process of law" clause of the State constitution.[55] Eventually, the act was sustained in holdings which confined its operation to property acquired by married women subsequent to its enactment. This result was based first on the Story-Kent principle that statutes may not be given a retrospective operation at the expense of vested rights, on the "obligation of contracts" clause, and on the "spirit of the constitution which declares" that "no person shall be deprived of life, liberty or property without due process of law." [56] Finally in Westervelt *v.* Gregg, decided in 1854, the same result was established by the recently created Court of Appeals squarely and explicitly on the "due process" clause.[57]

The real tussle with the reforming tendencies of the period was still to come. During the decade 1846 to 1856 no fewer than sixteen states passed antiliquor laws of a more or less drastic character. Not since the doctrine of vested rights had been formulated had such objectionable legislation from the standpoint of that doctrine been enrolled upon the statute books. How was it to be withstood? Some of the earlier of these laws took the form of local-option measures, and to meet them a new dogma of

---

[55] 4 Barb. (N.Y.), 295 (1847); 5 Barb. 474 (1849).
[56] Perkins *v.* Cottrell, 15 Barb. 446 (1851).
[57] 12 N.Y. 209 (1854).

constitutional law, drawn originally from John Locke's second *Treatise on Civil Government*, was contrived, the doctrine that the legislature cannot delegate its power— an absurd doctrine in this application of it, and one which was in singular contradiction both with legislative practice and with judicial decision anterior to 1846.[58] Furthermore, as was immediately shown, it was frequently an entirely futile doctrine; for the easy retort of the reforming legislatures was state-wide prohibition.

Such a law was enacted by the New York legislature in 1855. It forbade all owners of intoxicating liquors to

[58] The courts to whose fertility of mind this doctrine is primarily due were those of Delaware and Pennsylvania. See Rice v. Foster, 4 Harr. (Del.), 479 (1847), and Parker v. Commonwealth, 6 Pa. St. 507 (1847). The doctrine is elaborately refuted in People v. Reynolds, 10 Gilman (Ill.) (1848); also in Bull et al. v. Read, 13 Gratt. (Va.), 78 (1855); and in Johnson v. Rich, 9 Barb. (N.Y.), 680 (1848), with which, however, cf. Barto v. Himrod, 8 N.Y. 483. The Pennsylvania court abandoned the doctrine in Locke's Appeal, 72 Pa. St. 491 (1871). For a very early Pennsylvania case in which the doctrine was offered to the court but ignored, see 2 Yeates (Pa.), 493 (1799). An early Massachusetts case in which the same idea was brought forward but specifically repelled by the court is Wales v. Belcher, 3 Pick. (Mass.), 508 (1827). The immediate responsibility for this absurdity must fall to Chief Justice Gibson, a whimsical and erratic jurist. See 5 W. & S. (Pa.), 281 (1843). The passage from Locke's *Treatise on Civil Government* is § 141, which may owe something to a maxim of Coke's, *"delegata potestas non potest delegari."* 2 Inst. 597. Coke himself makes no mention of it in the Case of the Proclamations, where a sweeping delegation by Parliament to Henry VIII was, in effect, nullified. 12 Co. 74 (1610). For learned comment on the Cokian form of the maxim, see the article by Patrick Duff and Horace E. Whiteside in 14 *Cornell Law Quarterly* 168 ff. (1929); *Selected Essays on Constitutional Law* (Univ. of Chicago Press, 1938), IV, 291–316. Today the question of the validity of the referendum is a dead issue and the question of the delegability of legislative power is raised—when it is raised—with reference to grants of power to administrative bodies or, in the national forum, to the President.

sell them under any conditions save for medicinal purposes, forbade them further to store such liquors when not designed for sale in any place but a dwelling house, made the violation of these prohibitions a misdemeanor, and denounced the offending liquors as nuisances and ordained their destruction by summary process. In the great case of Wynehamer *v.* State of New York,[59] which

[59] 13 N.Y. 378–488 (1856). The followng passages from the controlling opinions indicate the line of reason taken: "All property is alike in the characteristic of inviolability. If the legislature has no power to confiscate and destroy property in general, it has no such power over any particular species." "The public good is in nothing more essentially interested than in the protection of every individual's private rights, as modeled by the municipal law." "In a government like ours, theories of public good or public necessity may be so plausible, or even so truthful, as to command popular majorities. But whether truthful or plausible merely, and by whatever numbers they are assented to, there are some absolute private rights beyond their reach, and among these the constitution places the right of property." "The act is one of fierce and intolerant proscription. It is unlawful to sell intoxicating liquors, to keep them for sale, or with intent to sell, and, with an exception of no importance to the question, it is to keep them at all. (§ 1.) They are declared a public nuisance (§ 25). . . ." "The act by no means waits for the operation of this machinery. Itself pronounces the sentence of condemnation, and the judicial machinery, such as it is, which it provides are agencies merely to insure the execution of the sentence. Property is lost before the police are in motion, and, I may add, crime is committed without an act or even an intention." "As property, the right to sell them is denied, and their commercial value is thus annihilated. They are, moreover, devoted to physical destruction." "To say, as has been suggested, that 'the law of the land,' or 'due process of law,' may mean the very act of legislation which deprives the citizen of his rights, privileges or property, leads to a simple absurdity." "It is plain, both upon principle and authority, that these constitutional safeguards, in all cases, require a judicial investigation, not to be governed by a law specially enacted to take away and destroy existing rights, but confined to the question whether, under the preexisting rule of conduct, the right in controversy has been lawfully acquired and is lawfully possessed." "Nor can I find any definition of property which does

comprises a new starting point in the history of due process of law, this act was overturned on the ground that the harsh operation of the statute upon liquors in existence at the time of its going into effect comprised an act of destruction not within the power of government to perform, *"even by the forms which belong to due*

---

not include the power of disposition and sale, as well as the right of private use and enjoyment." "The statute under consideration, without reference to its provisions for the seizure and physical destruction of intoxicating liquors, by force of its prohibitions alone, sweeps them from the commerce of the state, and thus annihilates the quality of sale, which makes them valuable to the owner. This is destructive of the notion of property." "When a law annihilates the value of property, and strips it of its attributes, by which alone it is distinguished as property, the owner is deprived of it according to the plainest interpretation, and certainly within the spirit of a constitutional provision intended expressly to shield private rights from the exercise of arbitrary power." "It is an entire misconception of the law itself to say that the species of property to which it relates is *forfeited by a violation* of its provisions. It is simply *extinguished* by the force of the prohibitions themselves." "There is no offence, except the misfortune of being the owner." "The form of this declaration of right, 'no person shall be deprived of life, liberty or property, without due process of law,' necessarily imports that the legislature cannot make the mere existence of the rights secured the occasion of depriving a person of any of them, even by the forms which belong to 'due process of law.' For if it does not necessarily import this, then the legislative power is absolute." "To provide for a trial to ascertain whether a man is in the enjoyment of either of these rights, and then, as a consequence of finding that he is in the enjoyment of it, to deprive him of it, is doing indirectly just what is forbidden to be done directly, and reduces the constitutional provision to a nullity. For instance, a law that any man who, after the age of fifty years, shall continue to live, shall be punished by imprisonment or fine, would be beyond the power of the legislature." "This scheme taken together, in my judgment, is a scheme not of regulation, but of legal destruction of property, which, as much as any other, was under the protection of the constitution." "The portion of the law which authorizes the seizure and destruction of liquor, where the prosecution or conviction of the owner is not contemplated, I should not hesitate

process of law." [60] The significance of this statement of
the issue is manifest. In every previous case of due process
of law the court had been able to treat a civil enactment
as, in certain applications, a bill of pains and penalties. In
Wynehamer *v.* State of New York, however, the court
was confronted with a frankly penal statute which provided a procedure, for the most part unexceptionable, for
its enforcement. That statute was nonetheless overturned
under the "due process of law" clause, which was
thereby plainly made to prohibit, regardless of the matter
of procedure, a certain kind and degree of exertion of
legislative power altogether. The result serves to throw
into strong light once more the dependence of the derived notion of due process of law upon extraconstitutional
principles; for it is nothing less *than the elimination of
the very phrase under construction from the constitutional clause in which it occurs.* The main proposition of
the decision in the Wynehamer case is that the legislature
cannot destroy by any method whatever what by previous law was property. But why not? To all intents and
purposes the answer of the court is simply that "no person shall be *deprived* of life, liberty or *property.*"

---

to pronounce void, as property is thus destroyed or the citizen deprived of it without process of law. It is not pretended, nor can it be,
that property which is not *per se* a nuisance can be annihilated by force
of a statute alone, or by proceeding *in rem* for the punishment of a
personal offence. Liquor is not a nuisance *per se*, nor can it be made so
by a simple legislative declaration. It does not stand in the category
of common nuisances which of themselves endanger the welfare or
safety of society. It is its use and abuse as a beverage which gives it
its offensive character. Otherwise it is entirely inoffensive. In my judgment, therefore, it cannot be confiscated to prevent its misuse, except
through a prosecution against the owner *in personam.*"

[60] *Ibid.*, 420 (my italics).

Thus was the doctrine of vested rights grappled to the written constitution firmly and unambiguously. Indeed, it was a question whether it had not been grappled so firmly as to have been throttled. This possibility was suggested by Judge T. A. Johnson in a dissenting opinion in which he attempted to reduce the decision to an absurdity. "It might," he asserted, "be urged with precisely the same pertinency and force, that a statute which prohibits certain vicious actions and declares them criminal deprives persons of their liberty and is therefore derogatory of the constitution." [61] In other words, the "due process" clause is just as potent a restraint on legislative power in relation to "liberty" as it is in relation to "property," a deduction capable of undermining all legislative power. The suggestion was given further point by the fact that three of the majority judges had not stopped with condemning the prohibition act because of its decreeing the physical destruction of existing stocks of liquor, but also because of its taking away their *vendability*, although in previous cases invoking the doctrine of vested rights it had been the *title* to property or its *physical possession* which had usually furnished the constitutional issue.

What, then, was the way out of this dilemma? Curiously enough, Judge Comstock indicated one element of a solution, quite inadvertently no doubt, when, in supporting his contention that the term "property" as used in the "due process" clause included its vendability, he said, "We must be allowed to know what is known by all persons of common intelligence, that intoxicating liquors are produced for sale and consumption as a bever-

[61] *Ibid.*, 468.

age. . . ." [62] In these words we encounter the first assertion of a notion which has since become an important ingredient of today's flexible doctrine of due process. For if courts can take cognizance of notorious facts for the purpose of invalidating statutes, there is no logical reason why they may do the same thing for the purpose of sustaining them. I shall deal further with this matter in the following chapter.

Another feature of the Wynehamer decision worth a moment's attention is its dismissal of the doctrine of natural rights. The ungracious task fell also to Judge Comstock. Conceding that "high authority" had been cited in support of the proposition that the State legislature was restricted not only by the written constitution but by "the fundamental principles of liberty" and "common reason and natural rights," Comstock expressed aversion to entering upon any such inquiry at a time when theories, alleged to be founded in natural reason and inalienable rights, but subversive of the necessary powers of government attracted the belief of considerable classes of men, and when too much reverence for government and law was certainly the least of the perils to which our institutions were exposed. Nor in fact was any such inquiry essential, "there being no process of reasoning by which it could be demonstrated that the Act for the Prevention of Intemperance, Pauperism and Crime was void upon principles and theories outside the Constitution, which would not also, and by an easier deduction, bring it in direct conflict with the constitution itself." [63]

[62] *Ibid.*, 387.
[63] *Ibid.*, 390–92; also Justice A. S. Johnson's opinion, *ibid.*, 410–13. Both Justices, however, save the principle of the separation of powers

It was Judge Comstock's belief, in short, that the protection of the "due process" clause could be confined to vested rights. Judge Johnson, pointing to the fact that the clause protected "liberty" as well as "property," took, as we have seen, the contrary view, and history has subsequently vindicated his prevision. Both judges, moreover, overlooked the potentialities of the word "property" itself. Yet Locke had written more than two centuries earlier that "every man has a 'property' in his 'person,'" a theme that James Madison had enlarged upon a century later: "This term ['property']," said Madison, "in its particular application means 'that dominion which one man claims and exercises over the external things of the world, in exclusion of every other individual.' But in its larger and juster meaning, it embraces everything to which a man may attach a value and have a right; and which leaves to every *one else the like advantage*. In the former sense, a man's land, or merchandise, or money is called his property. In the latter sense, a man has property in his opinions and a free communication of them. He has a property of peculiar value in his religious opinions, and in the profession and practice dictated by them. He has property very dear to him in the safety and liberty of his person. He has an equal property in the free use of his faculties and free choice of the objects on which to employ them. In a word, as a man is said to have a right to his property, he may be equally said to have a property

as a judicially enforcible limitation on "legislative power"; and see to the same effect Sill *v.* Corning, 15 N.Y. 297; People *v.* Draper, 15 N.Y., 532; and Sharpless *v.* Philadelphia, 21 Pa. St. 147 (1853), in which the Pennsylvania court adopted the doctrine of Taylor *v.* Porter.

in his rights. . . ." A hundred years after Madison the Supreme Court of the United States adopted and adapted these words to its interpretation of the "due process" clause of the Fourteenth Amendment.[64]

To return to the Wynehamer case: the Court of Appeals' decision produced an even more serious rift in the American Bench and Bar than had the decision of the Supreme Court twenty years prior to this in the Charles River Bridge case. In only one other State, Indiana, was a prohibition statute unqualifiedly held void, and there the decision, by a divided court, was based on the contention that the right to manufacture, the right to sell, and the right to drink spirituous liquors were "inalienable rights." [65] In all other States where the issue was raised the power of the legislature to restrict the liquor traffic was broadly asserted, often in the name of the "police power." The Vermont Supreme Court, pointing out that "the right to life, liberty, and property" all stood on a level in the State constitution, continued, "and certainly the two former are as sacred as the latter, although they have not seemed at all times to have called out the same legal acumen in their behalf. . . ." [66] A contemporary

[64] *Writings* (Hunt ed.), VI, 101–103. Cf. 165 U.S. at 589 (1897).

[65] Beebe *v*. St., 6 Ind. 501 (1855). This decision was overturned seven years later in Jackson *v*. St., 19 Ind. 312 (1862). In the latter case the court makes an interesting application of the doctrine of "judicial notice," stating that it does not know judicially that wine is not intoxicating and accordingly will not question the right of the legislature to declare it to be so. Cf. 94 U.S. at 132 (1876); and 123 U.S. at 662 (1887).

[66] Lincoln *v*. Smith, 27 Vt. 328 (1854); see also *In re* Power, 25 *ibid.*, 261 (1853); and State *v*. Parker, 26 *ibid.*, 357. In 27 Vt. occurs also C. J. Redfield's oft-quoted opinion sustaining the power of the State to require that railway companies fence in their rights of way. He said:

decision of the Supreme Court of Illinois proceeded on similar lines. Natural rights were surrendered or qualified upon entering into society by being subjected to the police power of government, which neither "the framers of Magna Carta nor of the constitutions of the United States and the States intended to modify, abridge or destroy." To the contrary, the police power was a developing power, a power which unfolded with the in-

---

"This police power of the State extends to the protection of the lives, limbs, health, comfort, and quiet of all persons, and the protection of all property within the State. According to the maxim, *sic utere tuo ut alienum non laedas,* which being of universal application, it must, of course, be within the range of legislative action to define the mode and manner in which every one may so use his own as not to injure others." And again: By this "general police power of the State, persons and property are subjected to all kinds of restraints and burdens, in order to secure the general comfort, health, and prosperity of the State; of the perfect right in the legislature to do which, no question ever was, or, upon acknowledged general principles, ever can be made, so far as natural persons are concerned." 27 Vt. 140 (1854). Actually this language is not as sweeping as at first glance it may seem to be—the police power is still anchored to the *"sic utere tuo"* maxim. And substantially the same remark may be made as to Chief Justice Shaw's equally famous opinion in Commonwealth v. Alger: "We think it is a settled principle growing out of the nature of well-ordered civil society, that every holder of property, however absolute and unqualified may be his title, holds it under the implied liability that his use of it shall not be injurious to the equal enjoyment of others having an equal right to the enjoyment of their property, nor injurious to the rights of the community. All property in this Commonwealth is . . . held subject to those general regulations which are necessary to the common good and general welfare. Rights of property, like all other social and conventional rights, are subject to such reasonable limitations on their enjoyment as shall prevent them from being injurious, and to such reasonable restraints and regulations established by law as the legislature, under the governing and controlling power vested in them by the constitution may think necessary and expedient." 7 Cush. (Mass.), 53 (1851).

creasing complexity of society and the advance of social needs.[67] The Supreme Court of Michigan used language even more sweeping. "The whole sovereignty of the people," it said, "is conferred upon the different departments of government; what the judiciary and executive have not would seem from necessity to have been granted to the other; and that other must possess all the powers of a sovereign state except such as are withheld by the state constitution and such as are conceded to the general government. In that grant there are many powers that are not strictly legislative and which are essential to administrative government. If this department is limited as a law-making power, what is the limitation upon the exercise of those powers strictly administrative? . . . It must be conceded there is none." [68]

[67] Goddard v. Jacksonville, 15 Ill. 589 (1854); see also Jones v. People, 14 ibid. 196 (1852), where the opinion of the court is based in part on 5 How. 504.

[68] State v. Gallagher, 4 Gibbs (Mich.), 244 (1856); see also People v. Hawley, 3 ibid., 330 (1854). Two cases of earlier date present features of some interest: (1) Lunt's Case, 6 Greenlf. (Me.), 412 (1830), where the question was that of the constitutionality of Stat. 1821, c. 133, prohibiting the sale of certain liquors, except in certain modes. Said Chief Justice Mellen, apropos of the constitutional authority of the legislature to pass "reasonable laws and regulations," "in all cases where the legislature have the constitutional authority to pass a law, the reasonableness of it seems to be a subject for their decision." There may be exceptions, "but we are not disposed to consider them among the probabilities of legislation." (2) Austin v. St., 10 Mo. 591 (1847), where the question was that of the constitutionality of the act of 1843, restricting the granting of dram-shop licenses. Said the court: "The State legislatures have the power, unless there be something in their own constitutions to prohibit it, of entirely abolishing or placing under restrictions any trade or profession which they think expedient. Can there be any doubt that the legislature of Missouri might declare the practice of law or medicine an unlawful calling if they thought fit to,

Only Rhode Island's Supreme Court actually had the Wynehamer decision before it. There counsel in cases arising under a State-wide prohibition act attempted to fasten the New York holding to the "law of the land" clause of the local constitution. "It is obvious," said the court in answer, "that the objection confounds the power of the assembly to create and define an offense with the rights of the accused to trial by jury and due process of law . . . before he can be convicted of it." And again: "Pushed to its necessary conclusions the argument goes to the extent, that once make out that anything real or personal is property, as everything in a general sense is, and legislation as to its use and vendability . . . must stop at the precise point at which it stood when the thing first came within the protection of this clause of the constitution." [69] From the point of view both of history and of logic, this refutation of the Court of Appeals' version of the "due process" clause is conclusive.

A single endorsement the decision in Wynehamer v. the People received contemporaneously, but that was a resounding one. Exactly a twelvemonth after the Court of Appeals' deliverance, Chief Justice Taney handed down his famous opinion in Scott v. Sandford holding the Missouri Compromise void because of, among other things, its violation of the "due process" clause of the Fifth Amendment. "An act of Congress [the opinion reads] which deprives a citizen of the United States of his liberty or property merely because he came himself or brought his

do so . . . ? But we are not aware that there is any provision in our constitution which would prevent the legislature from prohibiting dram selling entirely." Cf. case cited in note 38 *supra*.

[69] State v. Paul, 5 R.I. 185 (1858); State v. Keeran, *ibid.*, 497. See also note 51 *supra*.

property into a particular territory of the United States and who had committed no offense against the laws could hardly be dignified with the name of due process of law." [70]

The extraordinary character of this pronouncement is shown by two circumstances: first, by the fact that counsel at the bar did not allude in the remotest way to any such restriction upon Congressional power; and, secondly, by the fact that at this point the Chief Justice carried with him only two of his associates, Grier and Wayne, both of whom presented short opinions accepting perfunctorily the Chief Justice's line of argument. Justices Daniel, Campbell, and Catron, also held the Missouri Compromise to have been unconstitutional but upon far different grounds, Catron appealing to the doctrine of the equality of the States, and Campbell and Daniel basing their case on Calhoun's doctrine of State sovereignty and the corollary doctrine that Congress was the mere agent of the States in the exercise of its delegated powers. [71]

[70] 19 How. 393, 450 (1857).

[71] Curiously enough, the immediate source of the Chief Justice's dictum may have been the Republican platform of the year previous. See p. 114 *infra*. But the dictum was not entirely without basis in previous utterances from the Supreme Bench. As far back as 1819 Justice Johnson had used cryptic words in interpreting the "law of the land" clause of the Maryland constitution: "As to the words from Magna Charta, incorporated into the constitution of Maryland, after volumes spoken and written with a view to their exposition, the good sense of mankind has at length settled down to this: that they were intended to secure the individual from the arbitrary exercise of the powers of government, unrestrained by the established principles of private rights and distributive justice." Bank of Columbia *v.* Okely, 4 Wheat. at 244.

Much more nearly apposite, however, are Justice Henry Baldwin's words in Groves *v.* Slaughter, decided in 1841: "As each State has plenary power to legislate on this subject, its laws are the test of what

At no other point is Justice Curtis' dissent more convincing than in his refutation of this use of the term "due process of law." If, he inquired, the Missouri Compromise did indeed comprise one of a class of legislative enactments proscribed by the Fifth Amendment, what was to be said of the Ordinance of 1787, which Virginia and other states had ratified notwithstanding the presence of similar clauses within their constitutions; and what of the act Virginia herself passed in 1778, which prohibited the further importation of slaves? What, indeed, was to be said of the Act of Congress of 1808 prohibiting the slave trade, and the assumption of the Constitution that Congress would have that power without its being specifically bestowed, but simply as an item of its power to regulate commerce? And what was to be said of the Embargo Act of 1807 if the scope of Congressional authority to legislate within the limits of powers granted it was restricted by the Fifth Amendment, to say nothing

is property; if they recognize slaves as the property of those who hold them, they become the subjects of commerce between the States which so recognize them, and the traffic in them may be regulated by Congress, as the traffic in other articles; but no further. Being property, by the law of any State, the owners are protected from any violations of the rights of property by Congress, under the Fifth Amendment of the Constitution. . . . It follows, likewise, that any power of Congress over the subject is, as has been well expressed by one of the plaintiff's counsel, conservative in its character, for the purpose of protecting the property of the citizens of the United States, which is a lawful subject of commerce among the States, from any State law which affects to prohibit its transmission for sale from one State to another, through a third or more States." 15 Pet. at 514–16. And in Bloomer v. McQuewan et al., we find Chief Justice Taney himself, as spokesman for the Court, using the following language in sustaining, in 1853, the rights of a licensee of a patent under the patent laws: "And if such could be the interpretation of this law, the power of Congress to pass

of a recent decision of the Court itself upholding in principle the claim of power represented by that act? [72]

The fact of the matter is, as these questions serve to demonstrate, that Taney's opinion not only ratifies the Court of Appeals' holding, but considerably extends it. For not only is the right it protects, namely, that of a

---

it would be open to serious objections. For it can hardly be maintained that Congress could lawfully deprive a citizen of the use of his property after he had purchased the absolute and unlimited right from the inventor, and when that property was no longer held under the protection and control of the General Government, but under the protection of the State, and on that account subject to State taxation.

"The 5th amendment to the Constitution of the United States declares, that no person shall be deprived of life, liberty, or property, without due process of law.

"The right to construct and use these planing machines had been purchased and paid for without any limitation as to the time for which they were to be used. They were the property of the respondents. Their only value consists in their use. And a special act of Congress, passed afterwards, depriving the appellees of the right to use them, certainly could not be regarded as due process of law.

"Congress undoubtedly have power to promote the progress of science and useful arts, by securing for limited times, to authors and inventors, the exclusive right to their respective writings and discoveries.

"But it does not follow that Congress may, from time to time, as often as they think proper, authorize an inventor to recall rights which he had granted to others; or reinvest in him rights of property which he had before conveyed for a valuable and fair consideration.

"But we forbear to pursue this inquiry, because we are of opinion that this special act of Congress does not, and was not intended to interfere with rights of property before acquired; but that it leaves them as they stood during the extension under the general law. And in this view of the subject, the appellant was not entitled to the injunction he sought to obtain, and the Circuit Court were right in dismissing the bill." 14 How. at 553–54 (1853). See also Appendix II, at p. 191.

[72] 19 How. at 620–27.

slaveholder to take his slaves into a territory, the product of an extreme refinement on the concept of "property," but the opinion also explicitly invokes the word "liberty" of the amendment. Despite which Curtis' dissent proved comparatively ineffective even with the extremest critics of the decision. Indeed, the Republican platform of 1856 had anticipated Taney in his conception of the "due process" clause, and, stressing the word "liberty" in it, had forged it into a weapon against the power of Congress to "give legal existence to slavery in any territory of the United States"; and in the platform of 1860, what was now heresy was reiterated. And when more than a decade later the Court in Hepburn v. Griswold set aside the Legal Tender Act of 1862 one of the grounds of the holding was that, applied retrospectively, the act deprived creditors of property "without due process of law"; while the later opinion of the Court in Knox v. Lee, in reversing Hepburn v. Griswold, sidestepped the issue.[73]

In less than twenty years from the time of its rendition the crucial ruling in Wynehamer v. the People was far on the way to being assimilated into the accepted constitutional law of the country. The "due process" clause, which had been intended originally to consecrate a *mode of procedure*, had become a constitutional test of ever increasing reach of *the substantive content of legislation*. Thus was the doctrine of vested rights brought within the constitutional fold, although without dominating it. For confronting it was the still-expanding concept of the

[73] 8 Wall. at 624 (1869); 12 Wall. at 551 (1871). Justice Strong wrote the majority opinion in the latter case. In his dissenting opinion in the Sinking Fund Cases (1878) he takes a very different line, basing his construction of the "due process" clause on Hoke v. Henderson. 99 U.S. at 737–38.

police power. How was the quarrel between the potentially immovable body and the potentially irresistible force to be adjusted? It is to this subject that we turn in the following chapter.

CHAPTER IV

LIBERTY UNDER THE FOURTEENTH AMENDMENT

IN 1868 the Fourteenth Amendment was added to the Constitution; that same year Thomas M. Cooley brought out his *Constitutional Limitations*, the most influential treatise ever published on American constitutional law. The concurrence of these two events was, as time has shown, of much more than chronological significance.

The first section of the Fourteenth Amendment reads: "All persons born or naturalized in the United States, and subject to the jurisdiction thereof, are citizens of the United States and of the State wherein they reside. No State shall make or enforce any law which shall abridge the privileges or immunities of citizens of the United States; nor shall any State deprive any person of life, liberty or property, without due process of law; nor deny to any person within its jurisdiction the equal protection of the laws."

Here, in the "due process of law" clause, was laid the foundation for the reception by the Supreme Court of the United States of the outstanding results of constitutional interpretation in the State jurisdictions prior to the Civil

War, while in Cooley's pages a systematic statement of those results was provided for the first time. The two chapters of the *Limitations* which are of interest to us are XI, which is entitled "Protection to Property by 'Law of the Land,' " and XVI which is entitled "The Police Power of the States." Thus was the national Supreme Court on the one hand invested with a new jurisdiction of untested potentialities over State legislative power, and on the other hand supplied, as it were, with a double set of answers, each duly authenticated by precedents, to all questions which were capable of arising within this jurisdiction touching the vital problem of the relation of legislative power to the property right.

Nor is this to imply that Cooley was an altogether unbiased commentator.[1] Indeed, he frankly avowed his intention of pushing certain views of his own as opportunity might offer. Stating in his Preface that he had "faithfully endeavored to give the law as it had been settled by the authorities rather than to present his own views," he added, nevertheless, that "he did not attempt to deny—what he supposed would be sufficiently apparent —that he had written in full sympathy with all those restraints which the caution of the fathers had imposed upon the exercise of the powers of government. . . . In this sympathy and faith he had written of jury trials and the other safeguards to personal liberty, of liberty of the press and of vested rights; and he had also endeavored to point out that there are on all sides definite limitations which circumscribe the legislative authority, independent

---

[1] For an excellent account of Cooley's constitutional creed, see Benjamin R. Twiss, *Lawyers and the Constitution* (Princeton Univ. Press, 1942), 18–41.

of the specific restrictions which the people impose by their State constitutions. But while not predisposed to discover in any part of our system the rightful existence of any unlimited power, created by the Constitution, neither, on the other hand, had he designed to advance new doctrines, or to do more than clearly and with reasonable conciseness to state the principles to be deduced from the judicial decisions."

The Supreme Court of the United States, however, was not yet prepared in 1868, nor for some years afterward, to yield itself to the leadership of Cooley and those who, including an important section of the American Bar, shared his views. This was because a controlling majority of the Court felt that the duty immediately before it was to prevent "the federal equilibrium" from being completely undermined by the Reconstruction program of the Radical Republicans. Of this program the Fourteenth Amendment was potentially the most important feature.

The debates in Congress on the amendment leave one in little doubt of the intention of its framers to nationalize civil liberty in the United States, primarily for the benefit of the freedmen, to be sure, but incidentally for the benefit of all.[2] This would be done, it was calculated, by converting State citizenship and its privileges and immunities into privileges and immunities of national citizenship. Then by section 5 of the amendment, which empowers Congress to enforce its other provisions by "appropriate legislation," that body would be made the ultimate authority in delimiting the entire sphere of private rights in

---

[2] See especially Horace Edgar Flack, *The Adoption of the Fourteenth Amendment* (Johns Hopkins Univ. Press, 1908), 55–97 and 210–77.

relation to the powers of the States, leaving to the Supreme Court an intermediate role in this respect. Would, however, the Court accept a merely intermediate role? Wittingly or unwittingly, the Court, in fighting the battle for the "federal equilibrium," was fighting its own battle as well.

The amendment first came before the Court for elucidation in 1873 in the famous Slaughter House Cases.[3] The question at issue was the validity of an act of the Louisiana legislature which created a corporation called "The Crescent City . . . Company," and endowed it with the exclusive right to slaughter animals for food in the city of New Orleans. The butchers who had been left out of the arrangement, and were forced by it to resort to company's abattoirs to get their slaughtering done, at once raised the charge of "monopoly" and consequent unconstitutionality. Resident in New Orleans in 1873 was the Honorable John A. Campbell, who at the time of the Dred Scott case was a member of the Supreme Court, but who had later resigned his post when his home State, Alabama, left the Union. A current saying advised people in need of help to "turn to God and Mr. Campbell"; and this the disgruntled butchers of New Orleans promptly did, though in the end unavailingly. After hearing the case argued twice the Justices sustained the challenged legislation by a vote of 5 to 4. One is reminded of salty John Selden's identification of God with "the odd man."

For all that, Campbell's argument remains to this day

[3] 16 Wall. 36. On the continued good standing of the Court's construction in the Slaughter House Cases of the "privileges and immunities" clause, see United States v. Wheeler, 254 U.S. 281 (1920), and Madden v. Kentucky, 309 U.S. 83 (1940).

a notable event in the history of American constitutional law.[4] He launches it with a statement from a work by Thiers on *Property* which, in light of later developments, should be quoted: "The right to one's self, to one's own faculties, physical and intellectual, one's own brain, eyes, hands, feet, in a word to his soul and body, is an incontestable right; one of whose enjoyment and exercise by its owner no one can complain, and one which no one can take away."

From the platform thus provided him Campbell next proceeds to hurl a terrific attack against "monopoly," in the course of which Turgot, De Tocqueville, Buckle, Lieber, Sir George Cornwall Lewis, Macaulay, Sir John Culpeper's speech in the Long Parliament, and Coke's report of the Case of the Monopolies in 1601 are all successively laid under requisition. Turning then to the Thirteenth and Fourteenth Amendments, Campbell rejects with emphasis the notion that they were adopted solely, or even chiefly, for the purpose of securing the freedmen their rights. This result, while no doubt beneficial, was only incidental to a broader purpose, that of giving constitutional embodiment to the principle of "laissez-faire individualism which had been held by the colonists ever since they came to this soil." "What," he asked, "did the colonists and their posterity seek for and obtain by their settlement of this continent . . . ? *Freedom, free action, free enterprise—free competition.* It was in freedom they expected to find the best auspices for

---

[4] Two interesting accounts of Campbell's argument are "The Path of Due Process of Law" by Walton Hamilton in *The Constitution Reconsidered* (Conyers Read, ed.; Columbia Univ. Press, 1938), 170–75; and Twiss, *Lawyers and the Constitution*, 42–62.

every kind of human success." The Crescent City Company's monopolistic charter nullified this purpose. It placed a "servitude" on the backs of the butchers of New Orleans, it abridged the "privileges and immunities of citizens of the United States," it deprived persons of their "liberty," and denied them the "equal protection of the laws," that is to say, "equal protection *from* the laws." [5]

As has been mentioned, a closely divided Court rejected Campbell's argument and that of his associates. Said Justice Miller, speaking for the majority, "The one pervading purpose" of all of the recent amendments was "the freedom of the slave race . . . and the protection of the newly made freemen" [6] in their rights as citizens, and it was as far as possible from the intention of the Fourteenth Amendment to revolutionize the federal character of the Union or make "this Court a perpetual censor" on all State legislation affecting civil rights. The amendment's opening clause recognized and reiterated the distinction which had always existed between United States and State citizenship; and by the same token, the succeeding clause must be understood as distinguishing "the privileges and immunities of citizens of the United States" from those of State citizenship. The former comprised only such as owed "their existence to the Federal Government, its national character, its Constitution or its laws," and were comparatively few in number, the right to protection abroad, the right to visit the seat of government, "the right to engage in interstate and foreign commerce," and the like. The really fundamental privileges and immunities, the right to own property, to pursue one's livelihood, to contract, still remained what they

[5] 16 Wall. 45–57 *passim.*   [6] *Ibid.,* 71.

had always been, those of State citizenship and of State citizenship alone. Justice Miller then quoted a definition of the terms "privileges and immunities of citizens of the several States" of Article IV, section 2, of the Constitution which Justice Washington had made a half century earlier.[7] Oddly enough, when section 1 of the amendment was first introduced into the Senate, its official sponsor, Senator Howard of Michigan, being asked to elucidate the words "privileges and immunities of citizens of the United States," had quoted this identical passage from Justice Washington's opinion! [8]

As to the arguments of plaintiff's counsel based on the "due process" and "equal protection" clauses of the amendment, these, Justice Miller curtly observed, had "not been much pressed." It was "sufficient to say that under no construction" of the "due process" clause "that we have ever seen, or any that we deem admissible" could the Louisiana legislation under challenge "be held to be a deprivation of property." Likewise, "we doubt very much whether any action of a State not directed by way of discrimination against the negroes as a class, or on account of their race, will ever be held to come within the purview" of the "equal protection" clause.[9]

This casual dismissal by Justice Miller of the "due process" and "equal protection" clauses did not long remain the law of the Court, as we shall soon discover. His interpretation of the "privileges and immunities" clause of the amendment, on the other hand, stands substantially

---

[7] *Ibid.*, 73–80. The case referred to was Corfield *v.* Coryell, 4 Wash. C.C. 371; *Federal Cases,* No. 3,230 (1823).

[8] Flack, *Adoption of the Fourteenth Amendment,* 84–85.

[9] 16 Wall. 80–81. Cf. 113 U.S. 27 (1885); and 118 U.S. 356 (1886).

unimpaired to this day; and what it did was to obliterate that clause to all practical intents and purposes from the amendment. That this is so becomes evident on a moment's reflection. For if the "privileges and immunities of citizens of the United States" are confined to those privileges and immunities which arise immediately from other provisions of the Constitution or from national power constitutionally exercised, then such privileges and immunities were already fully safeguarded against State abridgment by the principle of the supremacy of the Constitution and of acts of Congress made "in pursuance thereof." The scores of cases in which the right to engage in interstate commerce has been vindicated against State legislation without any reference to the Fourteenth Amendment illustrate the point, as indeed does the entire history of constitutional interpretation both prior to and since the adoption of the amendment.

So devastating a result from a single act of judicial interpretation of a constitutional clause, obviously, is not to be squared with the conventional theory that the controlling purpose of judicial interpretation of statutes is to realize the intention of the lawmaker. But if we dismiss this theory from mind and take the position that a court is entitled to make what it can out of the words of a statute to the end of shaping it into an instrument of general good—that is to say, of the court's *view* thereof —then Justice Miller's highly ingenious piece of exegesis becomes more defensible. Furthermore, it has to be conceded that the potential revolution in our constitutional system which sections 1 and 5 of the amendment originally imported—and which has been partially realized subsequently—had, thanks to the more exciting character of the issues raised by other sections, largely escaped popular attention. Besides which, even the formal assent of a good third of the country had been essentially a coerced one.

Faced with this situation the majority of the Court felt that its duty lay in endeavoring to assimilate the amendment to the constitutional system as a whole, as it had come down from the past, and particularly to the principle of dual federalism. A powerful and highly vocal minority of the Court believed, on the other hand, that its duty lay in a very different direction—the direction pointed out by Campbell and his associates, and by Cooley, whom they repeatedly cited. The opinions in which this minority gave voice to the faith that was in them are among the most important utterances of this character ever to have emanated from the Supreme Bench.

The first of them was the work of Justice Field, who reiterated with emphasis Campbell's contention that the monopolistic character of the legislation before the Court rendered it violative not only of the Fourteenth Amendment but of the Thirteenth Amendment as well. "If exclusive privileges of this character," Field wrote, "can be granted to a corporation of seventeen persons, they may in the discretion of the legislature be equally granted to a single individual. If they may be granted for twenty-five years, they may be equally granted for a century, or in perpetuity," and if for one calling, then for all.[10] What Professor Powell has termed "the parade of horribles" had begun.

But Field's principal reliance was on the "privileges and immunities" clause. The Fourteenth Amendment

[10] *Ibid.,* 89.

"was intended," he asserted, "to give practical effect to the Declaration of 1776 of inalienable rights, rights which are the gift of the Creator, which the law does not confer, but only recognizes"; and this the clause did by converting the fundamental rights of citizenship under any free government into those of United States citizenship, thereby placing them "under the guardianship of national authority." Nor was there any "more sacred right of citizenship than the right to pursue unmolested a lawful employment in a lawful manner," for "it is nothing more nor less than the sacred right of labor." Nor did this mean that the State might not regulate the pursuits and callings of its citizens for the purpose of promoting the public health, good order, and general prosperity of society; but such regulations must apply equally to all and not establish exclusive privileges.[11]

But the really important opinion on this occasion from the point of view of later developments is Justice Bradley's. While, like Field, Bradley set out from the Declaration of Independence, he speedily found his way to firmer ground. "Rights to life, liberty, and the pursuit of happiness," he wrote, "are equivalent to rights of life, liberty and property. These are the fundamental rights which can only be taken away by due process of law, and which can only be interfered with or the enjoyment of which can only be modified by lawful regulations necessary or proper for the mutual good of all." "For the preservation, exercise and enjoyment of these rights the individual citizen, as a necessity, must be left free to adopt such calling, profession or trade as may seem most conducive to that end. Without this right he cannot be

[11] *Ibid.*, 95, 98, 105–106, 110.

a freeman. This right to choose one's calling is an essential part of that liberty which it is the object of government to protect; and a calling, when chosen, is a man's property and right. Liberty and property are not protected where these rights are arbitrarily assailed. . . . In my view, a law which prohibits a large class of citizens from adopting a lawful employment, or from following a lawful employment previously adopted, does deprive them of liberty as well as property without due process of law. . . . Such a law also deprives the citizen of the equal protection of the laws, contrary to the last clause of the section." [12]

The notable feature of this opinion is its transference of emphasis from the "privileges and immunities" clause to the "due process" and "equal protection" clauses; and in this respect Justice Bradley's perception was shared by Justice Swayne. "Life, liberty, and property," wrote the latter, "are forbidden to be taken 'without due process of law' and 'equal protection of the laws' is guaranteed to all. Life is a gift of God, and the right to preserve it is the most sacred of the rights of men. Liberty is freedom from all restraints but such as are justly imposed by law. Beyond that line lies the domain of usurpation and tyranny. Property is everything which has an exchangeable value, and the right of property includes the power to dispose of it according to the will of the owner. Labor is property, and as such merits protection. The right to make it available is next in importance to the rights of life and liberty. It lies to a large extent at the foundation of most other forms of property, and of all solid individual and national prosperity. 'Due process of law' is the applica-

12 *Ibid.*, 116, 122.

tion of the law as it exists in the fair and regular course of administrative procedure. 'Equal protection of the laws' places all upon a footing of legal equality and gives the same protection to all for the preservation of life, liberty and property and the pursuit of happiness." [13]

Throughout the three quarters of a century which has elapsed since the Slaughter House Cases were decided the history of the Fourteenth Amendment has been, in the main, the history of the Supreme Court's interpretation of the "due process" clause. Since, however, this is not a treatise in constitutional law our interest in the welter of cases and doctrines resulting from this activity will be confined to those which mark definite stages in the history of the expansion of the Court's supervision over the police power, this being the phase of State power which has in the past touched private rights most frequently and most vitally. More specifically, we shall be concerned mainly with two classes of cases: first, those which best illustrate the replacement of the doctrine of vested rights by judicial concern for less tangible interests; secondly, those in which principles that were originally restrictive of the Court's freedom of decision in this field of jurisdiction have been today largely replaced by nothing more definite than the Justices' "own sense of self-restraint."

The first case to be considered by the Court primarily on the basis of the "due process" clause of the amendment was Bartemeyer v. Iowa,[14] which was submitted in printed arguments at the time of the Slaughter House Cases, although it was not decided till a year later. The statute before the Court was a State-wide prohibition act, passed

[13] *Ibid.*, 127.   [14] 18 Wall. 129.

originally in 1851. Proponents of the act relied on Chapter XVI of Cooley's *Constitutional Limitations*, while the act's opponents staked their case on Chapter XI. The Court, speaking by Justice Miller, managed to steer a middle course. Although it was not the intention of the Fourteenth Amendment to deprive the States of their police power, said he, yet if a case were to come before the Court involving legislation which absolutely prohibited the sale of property owned when the legislation was enacted, a very grave question would be presented under the "due process" clause, a statement in support of which he cited Wynehamer *v.* the People. Fortunately the case at bar did not present this question, it being "absurd to suppose that the plaintiff, an ordinary retailer of drinks, could have proved in 1870 . . . that he had owned that particular glass of whiskey prior to the prohibitory liquor law of 1851"! The evasion here of the issue presented by the case, which was whether the Iowa statute had been void *ab initio* on account of its invasion of property rights, may have been technically arguable, but an evasion it remains for all that.[15]

The case bespeaks, in short, both the Court's recognition of the New York conception of the "due process" clause as illustrated in the Wynehamer case and the continued reluctance of a majority of its members to extend judicial review of State action by warrant of the new amendments. And in Loan Association *v.* Topeka,[16] decided a few months later, the same equivocal attitude persists. The

[15] See in this connection Justice Brandeis' opinion for the Court in Hamilton *v.* Ky. Distilleries Co., 251 U.S. 146, at 157–58 (1919). It was in this case that Wartime Prohibition was sustained in World War I.

[16] 20 Wall. 655 (1875); see also St. Louis *v.* Ferry Co., 22 Wall. 423, at 429 (1871); also pp. 67–68 *supra*.

constitutional issue concerned the right of a city council to tax its constituents in order to provide a bonus for a private manufacturing concern. The position of Justice Miller, again the Court's mouthpiece, was not rendered any easier by the fact that the Supreme Court of his home State, Iowa, had repeatedly given unqualified endorsement to the doctrine that a tax must be for a "public purpose" in the sense that the courts might give that term. But again, his astuteness contrived an escape from an embarrassing dilemma. Taking advantage of the circumstance that the case had come up through the circuit, he reverted to the practice of invoking extraconstitutional limitations which the Court had so ostentatiously abandoned a half-century earlier; and, citing Cooley's *Limitations* and an array of State decisions in which Chase's dictum in Calder *v.* Bull figured largely, he pronounced the Topeka ordinance void without reference to the Fourteenth Amendment. Justice Clifford dissented on the basis of Iredell's opinion in Calder *v.* Bull.

Despite the Court's disinclination to enter the field of jurisdiction to which the Fourteenth Amendment, even with the "privileges and immunities" clause stricken from it, still beckoned, it was being pressed by the Bar more and more insistently to do this very thing. Two years after the Topeka case it was asked, in the famous case of Munn *v.* Illinois,[17] to say that a statute which undertook to regulate the charges of grain elevators worked a deprivation of property without due process of law. A divided Court, speaking by Chief Justice Waite, a recent appointee to it, laid down the following propositions: First, the police power was akin to the power of the Brit-

[17] 94 U.S. 113 (1876).

ish Parliament, and the only restraints on it were those embodied in explicit prohibitions of the State and national constitutions.[18] In the second place, moreover, the common law itself recognized a category of businesses "affected with a public interest," whose charges it required should be "reasonable"; [19] and whether a business fell within this category was primarily for the legislature to determine, and judicial interference with such a determination was limited to those cases in which the Court was able to say of its own knowledge that "no state of facts could exist" to justify it.[20] Finally, the legislative determination of what rates and charges were "reasonable" in the case of a "business affected with a public interest" was not subject to judicial review. "For protection against abuses by legislation," the Chief Justice remarked sententiously, "the people must resort to the polls, not to the courts." [21]

Justice Field, for himself and Justice Strong, demurred with characteristic vehemence. The doctrine of the majority was "subversive of the rights of property" and of "liberty" too. The police power was not the equivalent of the power of Parliament; its exercise was confined to implementing the maxim *"sic utere tuo ut alienum non laedas."* There were no businesses "affected with a public interest" whose property ceased in consequence to be *"juris privati* only" except those which were recipients "of some special privilege" from the State, and Munn's business was not such a business. Earlier instances which the Court had adduced of legislative regulation of prices and charges had never been tested by "authoritative adjudication" and so were not persuasive.[22]

---

[18] *Ibid.,* 124.   [19] *Ibid.,* 125–30.   [20] *Ibid.,* 132–33.   [21] *Ibid.,* 134.
[22] See especially *ibid.,* 136, 140–41, 145, 152.

The ultimate fate of Munn *v.* Illinois has been somewhat like that of the Slaughter House Cases. The doctrine that the police power extends to the regulation of charges in the case of businesses "affected with a public interest" has never been abandoned by the Court. Indeed, the limitation which the principle impliedly threw about the State's police powers has been discarded in recent years.[23] The proposition, on the other hand, that the legislature's determination that certain charges are "reasonable" was not subject to judicial review has been, as to the question of their reasonableness for owners, abandoned long since. Chief Justice Waite himself laid the ax to the roots of this proposition within a decade, when in the midst of an opinion for the Court sustaining the right of a State to confer on a commission the power to regulate railway rates, he planted this dictum: "From what has thus been said, it is not to be inferred that this power of limitation or regulation is itself without limit. This power to regulate is not a power to destroy, and limitation is not the equivalent of confiscation. Under the pretense of regulating fares and freights, the State cannot require a railroad corporation to carry persons or property without reward; neither can it do that which in law amounts to a taking of private property for public use without just compensation, or without due process of law." [24] Three years later this dictum became, in effect, the law of the Court. Property even of a business "affected with a public use" is still

[23] The reference is to Nebbia *v.* N.Y., 291 U.S. 502 (1934), in which New York was sustained in its efforts to regulate the price of milk. The Honorable James M. Beck declared of the decision, with some exaggeration, however, that the Court had "calmly discarded its decisions of fifty years without even paying those decisions the obsequious respect of a funeral oration."

[24] Railroad Commission Cases, 116 U.S. 307, at 331 (1886).

private property, and as such is protected from confiscation by the doctrine of vested rights as embodied in the
"due process" clause of the Fourteenth Amendment.[25]
Meantime in Davidson v. New Orleans,[26] decided in
1878, the Court had unanimously sustained that city in
levying an assessment on certain lands to pay for the drain-
ing of near-by swamps. In addition, Justice Miller seized
the occasion to scold appellants for asking the Court to
review the determinations of the Louisiana authorities in
the name of the "due process" clause. "It is not a little
remarkable," said he, "that while this provision has been
in the Constitution of the United States, as a restraint
upon the authority of the Federal government, for nearly
a century, and while, during all that time, the manner in
which the powers of that government have been exercised
has been watched with jealousy, and subjected to the
most rigid criticism in all its branches, this special limitation upon its powers has rarely been invoked in the
judicial forum or the more enlarged theatre of public discussion. But while it has been a part of the Constitution
as a restraint upon the power of the States only a very
few years, the docket of this court is crowded with cases
in which we are asked to hold that State courts and State
legislatures have deprived their own citizens of life,
liberty, or property without due process of law. There
is here abundant evidence that there exists some strange
misconception of the scope of this provision as found in
the fourteenth amendment. In fact, it would seem, from
the character of many of the cases before us, and the
arguments made in them, that the clause under considera-

[25] Chicago, Milwaukee and St. Paul Ry. Co. v. Minn., 134 U.S. 418
(1890); Smyth v. Ames, 169 U.S. 466 (1898).   [26] 96 U.S. 97.

tion is looked upon as a means of bringing to the test of
the decision of this court the abstract opinions of every
unsuccessful litigant in a State court of the justice of the
decision against him, and of the merits of the legislation
on which such a decision may be founded. If, therefore,
it were possible to define what it is for a State to deprive
a person of life, liberty, or property without due process
of law, in terms which would cover every exercise of
power thus forbidden to the State, and exclude those
which are not, no more useful construction could be
furnished by this or any other court to any part of the
fundamental law."

Yet curiously enough, Justice Miller declined to follow up admonition with appropriate instruction. "Apart
from the imminent risk," said he, "of a failure to give any
definition which would be at once perspicuous, comprehensive, and satisfactory, there is wisdom, we think, in
the ascertaining of the intent and application of such an
important phrase in the Federal Constitution, by the
gradual process of judicial inclusion and exclusion, as the
cases presented for decision shall require, with the reasoning on which such decisions may be founded. This court
is, after an experience of nearly a century, still engaged
in defining the obligation of contracts, the regulation of
commerce, and other powers conferred on the Federal
government, or limitations imposed upon the States."

One wonders just how the Court expected to get the
opportunity to employ "the gradual process of judicial
inclusion and exclusion" unless the lawyers continued to
bring up cases! Justice Bradley, in a concurring opinion,
thought the majority narrowed "the scope of inquiry as
to what is due process of law" when property is taken

"more than it should. . . . Respect must be had," said he, "as to the cause and object of the taking," and if that was found to be "arbitrary, oppressive and unjust," declared not to be due process. Eighteen years later Bradley's view became that of the Court for this type of case.[27]

The group of cases just dealt with, therefore, left judicial review under the "due process" clause of the Fourteenth Amendment in a state of suspended animation. By a series of decisions in the October term of 1883 this situation was largely overcome and the Court at last put definitely on the way to unlimited review under the clause. The first of these were the Civil Rights Cases.[28] The question at issue was the validity of the Civil Rights Act of 1875 which made it an offense against the United States for innkeepers, common carriers, and theater managers to refuse admission or accommodation to persons "on account of race, color, or previous condition of servitude." A nearly unanimous Court set the act aside on the ground that Congress' power to legislate under section 5 of the amendment was only the power to disallow *positive* State action "already taken or impending"—a power possessed by the Court itself for the most part. The decision thus eliminated at one stroke any serious danger to the federal equilibrium from Congressional action under section 5, and by so doing opened the way at last for the Court to reconsider its own powers under section 1, and more especially under the "due process" clause.

Five months later, in deciding Hurtado v. California,[29] the Court gave clear indication of the new direction its

[27] Fallbrook Irrigation Dist. *v.* Bradley, 164 U.S. 112 (1896).
[28] 109 U.S. 3 (1883).   [29] 110 U.S. 516 (1884).

thought was taking. Plaintiff in error in the case, under sentence of death for murder, contended that since he had been brought to trial under a recently devised procedure which did not include indictment by grand jury, he was about to be deprived of life without "due process of law," and cited Coke in his behalf. The Court overruled the argument. The "due process" clause, said Justice Matthews, could not, in view of its pervasive operation upon *all* State powers be defined simply from the point of view of history. Let essential justice be observed, he continued, and "the law of the land of each State which derives its authority from the reserved and inherent powers of the State" is due process of law. "Arbitrary power," *per contra*, "enforcing its edicts to the injury of the persons and property of its subjects, is not law, whether manifested as the decree of a personal monarch or of an impersonal multitude. And the limitation imposed by our constitutional law upon the action of the governments, both State and National, are essential to the preservation of public and private rights, notwithstanding the representative character of our political institutions. The enforcement of these limitations by judicial process is the device of self-governing communities to protect the rights of individuals and minorities, as well against the power of numbers as against the violence of public agents transcending the limits of lawful authority even when acting in the name and wielding the force of government." [30]

In short, the States were informed on the one hand that they were free to improve their laws of procedure without regard for ancient technicalities, and admonished on the other hand that *every species of State legislation,*

[30] *Ibid.,* 536.

*whether dealing with procedural or substantive rights,
was subject to the scrutiny of the Court when the question of its essential justice is raised.*

Two months later the Court again had before it the
monopoly which it had sustained in the Slaughter House
Cases.[31] This time the question at issue was the right of
the legislature of Louisiana to limit the privileges thus
granted by chartering a competing concern. A unanimous Court answered "yes"; but whereas the old majority,
still captained by Miller, held that the original charter
was repealable, the State being unable to surrender its
police powers in so important a matter as the public
health, Justices Field and Bradley, in concurring opinions, simply reiterated the doctrines of their former dissents, and the latter was joined by two new Justices in
his reiteration. So from being the mere protest of an out-
voted dissentient, Bradley's conception of "liberty," now
sharpened to "liberty of pursuit," became the doctrine of
an *affirming* opinion, and as such easily susceptible
of being represented as the doctrine of the Court itself.

Nor was the importance of this development slow to
appear. Less than eight months after the decision in the
Butchers' Union case the New York Court of Appeals
unanimously set aside a statute which forbade the manufacture of cigars in tenement houses on the basis of a decision in which the Bradley dissent spearheaded an argument compacted of references to Adam Smith's *Wealth
of Nations*, the Darwinian theory of struggle for existence,
an assertion by Cooley in his sixth edition that "Freedom

[31] Butchers Union Co. *v.* Crescent City Co., 111 U.S. 746 (1884).

. . . is the general rule and restraint the exception," and other congenial materials.[32] The example thus set by the Court of Appeals was, moreover, followed in steady succession by the high courts of Pennsylvania, Illinois, West Virginia, Massachusetts, Colorado, Kansas, Ohio, Missouri, and others. Just as after decision in Calder *v.* Bull the State judiciaries took over the task of defending vested rights against unjustifiable "retrospective" legislation, so now they took up the gauge in increasing numbers in behalf of "liberty of pursuit" or, as it soon came to be called, "liberty of contract," especially in the field of labor relations.[33]

Meantime, in 1878, the American Bar Association had been founded. Its birthplace was Chicago, a fact reflecting the animus of some of its founders toward the "barbarous" decision in Munn *v.* Illinois. The membership of the new organization comprised from the first the *haute noblesse* of the Bar. On its roster in its early years appeared such names as John A. Campbell, Thomas M. Cooley, John W. Cary, William M. Evarts, Joseph H. Choate, Christopher G. Tiedeman, John N. Jewett, Edward J. Phelps, John G. Johnson, Stanley Matthews, Henry B.

---

[32] *In re* Jacobs, 98 N.Y. 98 (1885); Twiss, *Lawyers and the Constitution*, 93–109.

[33] See *In re* Jacobs, 98 N.Y. 98 (1885); People *v.* Marx, 99 *ibid.*, 377 (1885); Godcharles *v.* Wigeman, 113 Pa. St. 431 (1886); Millet *v.* People, 117 Ill. 294 (1886); State *v.* Goodwill, 33 W. Va. 179 (1889); Commonwealth *v.* Perry, 155 Mass. 177 (1891); State *v.* Loomis, 115 Mo. 307 (1893); Braceville Coal Co. *v.* People, 141 Ill. 66 (1893), etc. All these cases are discussed at length by Roscoe Pound in "Liberty of Contract," *Selected Essays on Constitutional Law* (Chicago Foundation Press, 1938), II, 208–37. See also J. B. Thayer, *Cases on Constitutional Law* (1894), I, 918–44.

Brown, Benjamin R. Curtis, Louis D. Brandeis, Charles E. Hughes, David J. Brewer, William H. Taft, John M. Harlan, Horace H. Lurton, George Shiras, James C. Carter, John F. Dillon, William C. Guthrie, George H. Sutherland, James M. Beck, and others—two former Justices of the Supreme Court, ten future Justices, future Attorneys-General, and *one* future President.[34]

The Association soon became a sort of juristic sewing circle for mutual education in the gospel of *laissez faire.* Addresses and papers presented at the annual meetings iterated and reiterated the tenets of the new creed: government was essentially of private origin; the police power of the State was intended merely to implement the common law of nuisance; the right to fix prices was no part of any system of free government; "in the progress of society, there is a natural tendency to freedom"; the trend of democracy is always away from regulation in the economic field; "the more advanced a nation becomes, the more will the liberty of the individual be developed," and so on. In brief, the guaranties which the Constitution affords private rights were intended to supply, above all other things, a legal and political sanction to the laws of political economy and to the process of evolution as forecast by Herbert Spencer. *The country was presented with a new, up-to-date version of natural law.*[35]

---

[34] Twiss, *Lawyers and the Constitution,* 141–73.

[35] Note also the following judicial dicta: "The paternal theory of government is to me odious. The utmost possible liberty to the individual, and the fullest possible protection to him and his property, is both the limitation and duty of government." Justice Brewer, in Budd v. N.Y., 143 U.S. at 551 (1892). To the same general effect is his much earlier dissent in 7 Kan. 549, 555–56 (1871). The Budd case, while before the New York Court of Appeals, also elicited some strong

In 1886 Christopher G. Tiedeman published his *Treatise on the Limitations of the Police Powers*.[36] Essentially a revision of and a supplement to Cooley, the work speedily attained great reputation with the Bar. In a Preface which surpassed even that of his predecessor's great work in candor, Tiedeman avowed a crusading motive. Socialism, communism, and anarchism were "rampant throughout the civilized world," while in this country "the conservative classes" stood in constant fear of "an absolutism more tyrannical . . . than any before experienced by man, the absolutism of a democratic majority." "The principal object of the present work," he continued, "is to demonstrate by a detailed discussion of the constitutional limitations on the police power . . . that democratic absolutism is impossible in this country," provided popular reverence for our Constitution "is nourished and sustained by a prompt avoidance by the courts of any violations of their provisions, in word or in spirit."

This rising demand in professional circles for an indefinite extension of judicial review in the name of

laissez-faire views from Judge (later Justice) Peckham. The law there involved, fixing the charges of elevators, was, he asserted, a harking back to principles of the seventeenth and eighteenth centuries, and ignored "the more correct ideas which an increase of civilization and a fuller knowledge of the fundamental laws of political economy and a truer conception of the proper functions of government have given us today." Such legislation was "vicious in its nature and communistic in its tendencies." 117 N.Y. 1 at 47 (1889). Judge Gray was of a similar opinion: "By reason of the changed conditions of society and a truer appreciation of the functions of government, many things have fallen out of the range of the police power, as formerly recognized, the regulation of which would now be regarded as invading personal liberty." *Ibid.*, 21–22. See further p. 198 *infra*.

[36] Twiss, *Lawyers and the Constitution*, 122–27.

"liberty" and "due process of law" did not, to be sure, go entirely unopposed. In State *v.* Loomis,[37] in which in 1893 the Supreme Court of Missouri set aside an act requiring that miners be paid in lawful money and not in store checks, Justice Barclay delivered a notable dissenting opinion. The majority of the court, said he, had adopted a totally new formula for the determination of constitutional cases, namely "that some legislation is not to be considered as *prima facie* valid, but calls for a showing of 'specific' authority to sustain it," which amounted, "in substance to a declaration that statutes which seem to the Court unjust or unreasonable are not 'due process of law,' though not otherwise distinctly forbidden by the Constitution." Noteworthy too is the attitude of the then recently established *Harvard Law Review*, which under the influence of Professor James Bradley Thayer combated the new tendency at every opportunity.[38] Such

[37] 115 Mo. 307 (1893).

[38] An especially noteworthy contribution to the debate was C. E. Shattuck's "The True Meaning of the Term 'Liberty' in Those Clauses . . . Which Protect 'Life, Liberty, and Property,'" in 4 *Harvard Law Review*, 365–92 (1891). Here it is pointed out that the word "liberty" as used by Blackstone means simply, "personal liberty. . . . The power of locomotion, of changing situation," illegal restraint of which was redressible by an action for false imprisonment; and the writ of habeas corpus was its especial protection. See 1 *Bl. Comms.* 129–37. Professor Thayer's own often-cited article on "the Origin and Scope of the American Doctrine of Constitutional Law," 7 *Harvard Law Review*, 129 ff., was written to prove the thesis that the scope of judicial review is "narrow." The article attributes undue importance to judicial reiterations of the "clear case" and similar platitudes. Both these articles are republished in the *Selected Essays* cited in note 33 *supra*. See also 7 *Harvard Law Review*, 300 and 433 (1894).

A notable debate on the "New Canon of Constitutional Interpretation" occurred in 1892 in the pages of 32 (n.s.) *American Law Register*, between two members of the Philadelphia bar. Mr. Richard C. Mc-

opposition would have been more effective had it once occurred to its exponents to search more closely the pedigree of the "due process" clause, something which their unquestioning acceptance of the doctrine of vested rights as applied in the Wynehamer and similar cases precluded. For the most part, accordingly, they were constrained to concentrate their fire on the conception of "liberty," a ghostly target which easily absorbed their shafts without visible defacement. Thayer and those who

---

Murtrie was the attacking party. He wrote: "It is quite astonishing to note how men who have dealt with constitutional questions cannot see, or rather will not act on the plain rule that a constitutional question is, and must always be, so far as the Court is concerned, a question of *power*, not of *right*. . . . The most striking instance, however, of the loss of an anchorage in constitutional interpretation is to be seen in Budd *v.* New York (143 U.S. 517). A dissent of three judges shows that the case was warmly discussed. And yet, while the sole question was the power of a State to regulate prices charged by a grain elevator, not one person, counsel or court, seems to have started with the simple inquiry— Where is the clause in the Constitution which prohibits such a thing? On the contrary, time honored sentences from Magna Charta supposed to be embodied in the Constitution of the United States were the nature of the argument relied on. And all we can infer from the judgment is that it is not improper to apply the principles of the Magna Charta to exclude the power of the State to name prices for commodities or services. Yet who could ever suppose it to have such a meaning? It may be very disagreeable to accept the proposition that the legislature of a State can alter prices . . . , can regulate what we shall eat and what we shall drink and wherewithal we shall be clothed and what kind of business we shall engage in, but it is plain this is the case unless there is a restriction imposed by something that is not in the Constitution. . . . Is there anything more grotesque than the modern rule which overrides by implication the express words of the Constitution by calling this new functionary *the police power?* . . . [Note Mr. McMurtrie's realization of the *restrictive* connotation of the term "police power."] The climax is arrived at when the *inalienable right to life, liberty and the pursuit of happiness* is gravely contended to be a ground for refusing to enforce a statute, like this." McMurtrie con-

shared his views may, nevertheless, have been responsible, in part at least, for the fact that the Supreme Court of the United States lagged a full decade behind the generality of the State courts in taking up with the new doctrine.

I return to sketch the steps by which the Supreme Court, casting aside its reluctance to become "the per-

---

cludes: "We shall be met hereafter with . . . a new canon of constitutional law, viz., that *a statute interfering with natural rights must be shown to be authorized, not that it must be shown to be prohibited.*" McMurtrie was answered by William Draper Lewis. Expounding "The New Canon," Lewis wrote: "The habit of mind which makes one look to the Fourteenth Amendment as prohibiting States from passing laws which our forefathers would have called against 'natural rights,' and we, in the stricter parlance of modern political science call 'against the first principles of civil liberty,' springs . . . from regarding State constitutions as instruments for conferring, and not for taking away power. . . . This general attitude toward the interpretation of State constitutions tends to give the widest possible meaning to the words, to be found in the Bill of Rights of nearly all State constitutions, viz., 'due process of law' or 'the law of the land.'" The controversy between McMurtrie and the Supreme Court, Lewis continues, "is the old controversy between strict construction and liberal construction transferred to a new field, and in which many, as Mr. McMurtrie, who is a staunch defender of Federal power, have changed sides." The first century of constitutional development was taken up with the discussion of the division of power between State and Federal Governments, and the individual. And State rights were confused and the principles of individual liberty neglected. Thus from the death of Chief Justice Marshall men accepted without question the maxim that a State legislature had all power not expressly taken away from it by the National or State Constitutions. The sphere of civil liberty "involves the *next great question of constitutional law.*" In a second article, Mr. Lewis discussed the question "How Far Civil Liberty was Thought, Prior to 1816 to be Secured in Written Constitutions," citing Ham *v.* McClaws; *Federalist,* No. 44; Vanhorne's Lessee *v.* Dorrance; Calder *v.* Bull; Ogden *v.* Blackledge; University *v.* Foy; Fletcher *v.* Peck; Dash *v.* Vankleeck; Society *v.* Wheeler; Terret *v.* Taylor; The Dartmouth College case—all of which serves to exhibit very well the ancestry of the "New Canon."

petual censor" of State legislation, came at last to accept
unlimited judicial review under the "due process" clause
of the Fourteenth Amendment. Our attention is initially
claimed by the subject of "judicial notice." In his opinion
in the Wynehamer case Judge Comstock, pointing out
that it was a matter of general knowledge that intoxicants
were kept for sale, had applied this acknowledged fact
against the act under review. In Munn v. Illinois, Chief
Justice Waite gave the conception a diametrically opposed application, declaring in substance, that where the
validity of a legislative act depended on the existence of
certain facts, they must be presumed conclusively to
exist unless other facts of which the Court was entitled
to take notice showed the contrary.

Another facet of the subject was uncovered in 1887 in
the important case of Mugler v. Kansas,[39] which was another prohibition case. The Court sustained the act, but
accompanied its holding with a significant caveat. "It does
not at all follow," said Justice Harlan, "that every statute
enacted ostensibly for the promotion of these ends is to
be accepted as a legitimate exertion of the police power
of the State. There are, of necessity, limits beyond which
legislation cannot rightfully go. . . . The courts are not
bound by mere forms, nor are they to be misled by mere
pretenses. They are at liberty—indeed, are under a solemn
duty—to look at the substance of things, whenever they
enter upon the inquiry whether the legislature has tran-
scended the limits of its authority. If, therefore, a statute
purporting to have been enacted to protect the public
health, the public morals, or the public safety, has no real
or substantial relation to those objects, or is a palpable

[39] 123 U.S. 623.

invasion of rights secured by the fundamental law, it is the duty of the courts to so adjudge, and thereby give effect to the Constitution."

And how was the Court to determine whether a statute before it bore a "real and substantial relation" to acknowledged ends of the police power? "There is no justification," Justice Harlan answered, "for holding that the State [of Kansas] under the guise merely of police regulations, is here aiming to deprive the citizen of his constitutional rights; for we cannot shut out of view the fact, within the knowledge of all, that the public health, the public morals, and the public safety, may be endangered by the general use of intoxicating drinks; nor the fact, established by statistics accessible to everyone, that the idleness, disorder, pauperism, and crime existing in the country are, in some degree at least, traceable to this evil. . . ." [40]

This was a vastly different position from that of Waite in the Munn case in two respects. Gone was the broad conception in that case of the police power as analogous to the power of the British Parliament. To the contrary, it is here "cabined, cribbed, confined" to the protection of the "public health, safety, and morals"; and while the Court sustained the Kansas statute, it did so not because it did *not* know independently that justifying facts did *not* exist, but because it *did* know independently that they *did* exist, which implied the logical converse, that the Court was entitled to overturn a statute for which it lacked a justification of facts accessible to it by the rules governing judicial notice.

But did the Court really mean this? The question arose

[40] *Ibid.*, 661–62.

very speedily. The year following Mugler *v.* Kansas, the Justices were confronted in Powell *v.* Pennsylvania [41] with an act prohibiting the manufacture and sale of oleomargarine. Though no facts of sufficient notoriety for it to take cognizance of them were brought forward in justification of the statute, the Court, speaking again by Justice Harlan, nonetheless sustained it, saying: "It does not appear upon the face of the statute, or from any facts of which the Court must take judicial cognizance, that it infringes rights secured by the fundamental law." The statute was sustained, in short, on the principle of *presumed validity*.

A comparison of the Mugler and Powell cases for their bearing on the competing doctrines of *presumed validity* and of *judicial notice* plunges one at first into some perplexity, but once the hypothesis is adopted, which later developments will be seen to warrant, that neither case was regarded by the Court as stating an exclusive rule, then the subject clears up considerably. It was never the intention of the Court to put itself in bondage to either principle, but rather to resort to the one or the other depending on which one seemed best calculated to support a conclusion arrived at on other grounds. *Neither rule, in short, was meant to fetter freedom of judicial review under the "due process" clause, but rather to enlarge it.*

The question arises whether it is possible to demark the respective provinces of the two rules. At least in retrospect it is; *the principle of judicial notice as formulated in the Mugler case was eventually found to be well adapted to bolster the laissez-faire conception of "liberty" as non-*

[41] 127 U.S. 678.

interference by government in the economic sphere, and especially in the sphere of employer-employee relations. Outside this sphere the doctrine of presumed constitutionality still continued generally operative until after World War I.

The Court first invoked Bradley's conception of "liberty" to set aside a State enactment in Allgeyer *v.* Louisiana,[42] which was decided early in 1897, nearly ten years after the Mugler case. Why the delay? The answer is that down to 1887 the Court was still dominated by appointees to it during or shortly after the Civil War, men whose constitutional thinking was largely shaped by the burning issues of that period. Between 1888 and 1898, however, six replacements on the Supreme Bench took place, and five of the new appointees were the Justices who made up the majority which decided the Lochner case in 1905. They were products—the winnowed grain—of the Bar's self-indoctrination in the tenets of laissez-faireism.

The year following the Allgeyer case, Holden *v.* Hardy [43] was decided, the first case in which the Court was squarely confronted with an enactment dealing with the employer-employee relationship. Here was sustained by a vote of 7 to 2 a Utah statute limiting hours of labor in mines, the basis of the holding being the Court's recognition of the fact that work beneath the surface of the earth was attended by special dangers to health and had always been a subject of legislative solicitude more or less. At the same time, Justice Brown took pains to disavow for the Court any disposition "to criticize the many authorities which hold that State statutes restricting the

[42] 165 U.S. 578; cf. 157 U.S. at 165 (1894).   [43] 169 U.S. 366.

hours of labor are unconstitutional. . . . The question in each case," said he, "is whether the legislature has adopted the statute in the exercise of a reasonable discretion, or whether its action be a mere excuse for an unjust discrimination, or oppression, or spoliation of a particular class." [44]

Whence comes this challenging formula, "exercise of a reasonable discretion"? Justice Brown himself furnishes us the clue in the passage which he extracts from Chief Justice Shaw's famous opinion of nearly a half-century earlier in Commonwealth v. Alger.[45] This in turn is a paraphrase of that provision of the Massachusetts constitution of 1780 which, in words borrowed from the Provincial Charter of 1691, empowers "the general court" "from time to time, [to] make, ordain, and establish, all manner of wholesome and reasonable orders, laws, statutes, and ordinances. . . ." [46] And reaching back of this, and bringing us full circle to the dictum in Bonham's Case once more, is the common law's exaltation of the test of "reasonableness." [47]

[44] *Ibid.*, 397–98.
[45] *Ibid.*, 392. See also Brown's language in Lawton v. Steele, 152 U.S. 133, 137 (1894); also notes 66 and 68 of Chapter III *supra*.
[46] Thorpe, *American Charters, Constitutions* . . . , III, 1882 and 1894.
[47] Another avenue for the entry of the doctrine that legislation must be "reasonable," in some sense or other, was afforded by the terms in which power is usually conferred by State legislatures upon municipal corporations. A case in point, in which the doctrine in question was turned against the legislation under review, is that of Austin v. Murray, decided by the Massachusetts Supreme Judicial Court in 1834. The issue was the validity of a by-law interdicting the bringing of the dead into the town from abroad for purposes of burial, a prohibition which touched chiefly or exclusively Catholic parishioners. The court overturned the by-law as being "wholly unauthorized" by the act of

Instructive, too, is Justice Brown's endeavor to discover how the "due process" clause came to take on this significance—the more instructive for being so largely fruitless. From devoting some seven pages to a review of cases in which the "due process" clause was involved in its purely adjective sense, Brown suddenly steers the discussion into Justice Miller's cliché about "the gradual process of judicial inclusion and exclusion," and points to "the power to acquire property" as the source of the

---

the legislature, and as "an unreasonable infringement on private rights." Elaborating the latter point it said: "The illegality of a by-law is the same whether it may deprive an individual of the use of a part or of the whole of his property; no one can be so deprived unless the public good requires it. And the law will not allow the right of property to be invaded under the guise of a police regulation for the preservation of health when it is manifest that such is not the object and purpose of the regulation. . . . [This by-law] is a clear and direct infringement of the right of property without any compensating advantages, and not a police regulation, made in good faith for the preservation of health." 16 Pick. (Mass.), 121. Which is to say that the "rule of reason" was capable at times of mitigating the rigors of the doctrine of vested rights. There can be no question that it has often done so in the jurisprudence of the Supreme Court. Compare, e.g., the Wynehamer case and Mugler v. Kansas, where the test of "reasonableness" is invoked in different terms. "It is settled that neither the 'contract' clause nor the 'due process' clause has the effect of overriding the power of the State to establish all regulations that are reasonably necessary to secure the health, safety, good order, comfort, or general welfare of the community; that this power can neither be bargained away, and is inalienable even by express grant; and that all contract and property rights are held subject to its fair exercise." Justice Pitney for the Court in Atlantic Coast Line Co. v. Goldsboro, 232 U.S. at 558 (1914). Also, compare both opinions in Home Building and Loan Assoc. v. Blaisdell, 290 U.S. 398 (1934), where "emergency" is held by a narrow majority of the Court to bring moratorium legislation within the "rule of reason." See also Charles Grove Haines, The Revival of Natural Law Concepts (Harvard Univ. Press, 1930), 166-95, 232-34.

right to make contracts with that end in view. While this suggestion inferentially presents the doctrine of freedom of contract as a direct offspring of the doctrine of vested rights, it obviously throws no light at all on the course of reasoning by which the latter doctrine came to be read into the "due process" clause. A concluding reference to Allgeyer *v.* Louisiana deposits the learned Justice precisely at the point from which he set out.[48]

Lochner *v.* New York [49] bears much the same relation to Holden *v.* Hardy as the Powell case did to the Mugler case, but the result reached was the exact contrary. In the Mugler case the Court marched uphill; in the Powell case it marched down again. In the Lochner case there was no such retreat from the logical implications of the Holden case. The statute involved limited the work in bakeries to ten hours per day and sixty hours per week. A closely divided Court set the act aside because no justifying facts were properly accessible to judicial notice. The act was consequently stigmatized as a gratuitous interference in the contractual relations of persons *sui juris,* engaged in an ordinary pursuit, and hence not a permissible exercise of the police power.

"It must, of course, be conceded," said Justice Peckham, "that there is a limit to the valid exercise of the police power by the State. . . . Otherwise the Fourteenth Amendment would have no efficacy and the legislatures of the States would have unbounded power, and it would be enough to say that any piece of legislation was enacted to conserve the morals, the health or the safety of the people; such legislation would be valid, no matter how absolutely without foundation the claim might be. The

[48] 169 U.S. at 381–91.   [49] 198 U.S. 45 (1905).

claim of the police power would be a mere pretext,—become another and delusive name for the supreme sovereignty of the State to be exercised free from constitutional restraint. . . . In every case that comes before this court, therefore, where legislation of this character is concerned and where the protection of the Constitution is sought, the question necessarily arises: Is this a fair, reasonable and appropriate exercise of the police power of the State, or is it an unreasonable, unnecessary, and arbitrary interference with the right of the individual to personal liberty. . . ." Nor does this mean, Justice Peckham insists, that the Court is substituting its own judgment for that of the legislature. "If," he asserts, "the act be within the power of the State, it is valid, although the judgment of the Court might be totally opposed to the enactment of such a law. But the question would still remain: Is it within the police power of the State? And this question must be answered by the Court." [50]

Justice Harlan, speaking in dissent for himself and Justices White and Day, adduced the *Eighteenth Annual Report by the New York Bureau of Statistics of Labor*, a Professor Hirt's treatise on the *Diseases of the Workers*, and "another writer," who testified to the chronic suffering of bakers from inflamed lungs and bronchial tubes and from sore eyes, to their low resistance to diseases, and to their short average life. Thus the reasonableness of the enactment under consideration as a health measure was at any rate open to discussion, Harlan urged, and that fact of itself put it within legislative discretion.[51]

Justice Holmes's opinion, probing deeper, challenged the soundness of the concept of "liberty" on which the

[50] *Ibid.*, 56–57.　　　　　　　[51] *Ibid.*, 69–72. Cf. 197 U.S. 11.

decision rested. "This case," said he, "is decided on an economic theory which a large part of the country does not entertain. . . . The Fourteenth Amendment does not enact Mr. Herbert Spencer's Social Statics. . . . a constitution is not intended to embody a particular economic theory, whether of paternalism and the organic relation of the citizen to the State or of *laissez faire*. It is made for people of fundamentally differing views, and the accident of our finding certain opinions natural and familiar, or novel and even striking, ought not to conclude our judgment upon the question whether statutes embodying them conflict with the Constitution of the United States. . . . I think that the word 'liberty' in the Fourteenth Amendment is perverted when it is held to prevent the natural outcome of a dominant opinion, unless it can be said that a rational and fair man necessarily would admit that the statute proposed would infringe fundamental principles as they have been understood by the traditions of our people and of our law." [52] Yet even Justice Holmes did not, any more than the other dissentients, question the historical validity of the conception of "due process of law" on which the right of the Court to take the case reposed fundamentally.

Although the precise ruling in Lochner *v.* New York was reversed twelve years later in Bunting *v.* Oregon,[53] Peckham's opinion set a pattern, both as to doctrine and as to method, which still prevailed with the Court a generation later. Not that this pattern was always adhered to. One heard much during these years of "liberal" as opposed to "conservative" judges, and sometimes the one type and sometimes the other appeared to sway the Court,

[52] *Ibid.*, 75–76.   [53] 243 U.S. 426.

depending on the "malfeasances"—or benefactions—"of chance and the calendar." [54] The issue between the two schools was ordinarily the quarrel between the doctrine of the *presumed validity* of legislative acts and the doctrine illustrated by the Lochner case, that *in the realm of industrial relations a special burden of proof rested on the State.*

In 1908—to mention a few illustrative cases—the Court had before it an Oregon statute limiting the hours of women industrially employed to ten hours per day and sixty hours per week.[55] In support of the act, Mr. Louis D. Brandeis of Boston presented a brief in which "only two scant pages were given to conventional legal arguments" and over a hundred pages were devoted to a review of official and scientific opinion to the effect that long hours of labor were especially dangerous to women because of their physical organization and their maternal function. The Court, speaking by its most conservative member, Justice Brewer, ruled that these facts were sufficiently authenticated to permit it to take judicial notice of them, and on that ground, in part, sustained the act. But the Brandeis formula was soon found to be an untrustworthy reliance. In 1917 a comparable brief was presented the Court in support of a Washington statute which decreed the end of private employment agencies for gain.[56] Picking up the voluminous document, Chief Justice White remarked, that given time, he could easily compile one twice as thick to justify the outlawing of

[54] Thanks to Professor Powell.
[55] Muller *v.* Ore., 208 U.S. 412; Alpheus T. Mason, *Brandeis; A Free Man's Life* (1946), 248–54.
[56] Adams *v.* Tanner, 244 U.S. 590.

the legal profession! The act was disallowed by a vote of 6 to 3, one of the dissentients being Justice Brandeis. Six years later the Court overturned an act of Congress which created a commission with authority to prescribe minimum wages for women employed in the District of Columbia.[57] Adopting Cooley's axiom that "freedom of contract is the rule and restraint is the exception," Justice Sutherland, speaking for the Court, held that only a very special emergency could justify such a measure, and declined in light of the Nineteenth Amendment to treat the case of female workers as exceptional. In 1936, on the eve of the New Deal constitutional revolution, the Court further ruled—what had been generally taken for granted all along—that the 1923 holding applied also to State minimum-wage acts.[58]

Meanwhile two important developments, one procedural, one doctrinal, had occurred, the joint effect of which was to augment the scope of judicial review under the Fourteenth Amendment indefinitely. The procedural improvement was illustrated in Burns Baking Co. v. Bryan,[59] in which the Court set aside a Nebraska statute requiring bread sold in quantities to maintain a specified weight twenty-four hours after baking and allowing a tolerance in excess weight of two ounces per pound. While conceding the right of the State to protect purchasers against fraud by short weights, the Court declared the act before it "not calculated to effectuate that purpose" and the restrictions imposed by it upon bakers and sellers of bread, "essentially unreasonable and arbitrary," and

[57] Adkins v. Childrens Hospital, 261 U.S. 525 (1923).
[58] Morehead v. N.Y. ex rel. Tipaldo, 298 U.S. 587.
[59] 264 U.S. 504 (1924).

cited in support of this verdict an unprecedented range of facts. Thus, without a word of repining, the Court cast aside the trammels of "judicial notice," an act of independence which was rendered possible by the circumstance that the case was first brought in the State court on an application for an injunction against the governor of the State. The case thus came up to the Supreme Court accompanied by a copious finding of facts by the trial court bearing directly on the question of the act's "reasonableness." Some years earlier the Supreme Court would probably have considered itself disabled by the Eleventh Amendment from taking such a case, but since 1908 this method of testing the validity of State legislation even in the lower federal courts had gradually become accepted practice.[60]

Justice Brandeis' dissenting opinion takes equally broad range. Nor indeed is he averse to admitting that he has strayed into the legislative field; he only complains that the Court has done the same thing. The Court's holding, he asserts, "is in my opinion, an example of the powers of a super-legislature—not the performance of the Constitutional function of judicial review." Justice Brandeis evidently assumed that the presumed validity rule was still binding on the Court, while the majority thought otherwise.

The *doctrinal* extension of judicial review under the "due process" clause alluded to above was an outgrowth of World War I and comprised an enlarged conception of the "liberty" protected by the clause. The starting point was furnished by two decisions in 1923 in which the Court

[60] See discussion of this subject in Edward S. Corwin, *Twilight of the Supreme Court*, 80–84 and 208–209.

set aside as to private schools several State statutes forbidding the teaching of any modern language but English in the first eight grades.[61] Then in 1925 in the leading case of Gitlow *v.* New York [62] the Court declared itself prepared to "assume that freedom of speech and of the press, which are protected by the 1st Amendment from abridgment by Congress, are among the fundamental personal rights and 'liberties' protected by the due process clause of the 14th Amendment from impairment by the States." The Court sustained the statute under review, which forbade the advocacy of the overthrow of government by violence, on the Blackstonian principle that liberty of the press does not sanction utterances "tending" to corrupt public morals or to disturb the public peace.

[61] Meyer *v.* Neb., 262 U.S. 380.

[62] 268 U.S. 652; see also Charles Warren, "The New 'Liberty' under the Fourteenth Amendment," *Selected Essays* (1938), II, 237–66. In Patterson *v.* Colo., 205 U.S. 454 (1907), the Court speaking by Justice Holmes, said: "We leave undecided the question whether there is to be found in the Fourteenth Amendment a prohibition similar to that in the First. But even if we were to assume that freedom of speech and freedom of the press were protected from abridgment on the part not only of the United States but also of the States, still we should be far from the conclusion that the plaintiff in error would have us reach. In the first place, the main purpose of such constitutional provisions is 'to prevent all such *previous restraints* upon publications as had been practiced by other governments,' and they do not prevent the subsequent punishment of such as may be deemed contrary to the public welfare. Commonwealth *v.* Blanding, 3 Pick. 304, 313, 314; Respubica *v.* Oswald, 1 Dallas, 319, 325. The preliminary freedom extends as well to the false as to the true; the subsequent punishment may extend as well to the true as to the false. This was the law of criminal libel apart from statute in most cases, if not in all. Commonwealth *v.* Blanding, *ubi sup.;* 4 *Bl. Comm.* 150." This looks very like a complete ratification of Blackstone. However, as Justice Holmes remarks in the same opinion, "There is no constitutional right to have all general propositions of law once adopted remain unchanged." *Ibid.,* 461–62.

Justice Holmes, speaking also for Justice Brandeis, dissented on the basis of the proposition that to be banned constitutionally words must have been "used in such circumstances" and have been "of such a nature as to create a clear and present danger that they will bring about the substantive evils that the State has a right to prevent." In such fashion did "the clear and present danger" rule make its debut—a creation out of whole cloth, which today puts in the Court's hands a weapon against legislative restrictions on freedom of utterance closely comparable to that which the concept of "freedom of contract of persons *sui juris*" had since the Lochner decision furnished it against legislative interventions in the field of industrial relations.[63]

Commenting in 1937 on this enlargement of judicial review under the Fourteenth Amendment, Justice Cardozo wrote: Of freedom of thought and speech "one may say that it is the matrix, the indispensable condition, of nearly every other form of freedom. . . . So it has come about that the domain of liberty, withdrawn by the Fourteenth Amendment from encroachment by the states, has been enlarged by latter-day judgments to include liberty of the mind as well as liberty of action. The

[63] See Edward S. Corwin, "Freedom of Speech and Press under the First Amendment: A Résumé," *Selected Essays*, II, 1060–68. It is to be noted that Justice Holmes, in justifying to Sir Frederick Pollock his dissent in Abrams *v.* U.S., 250 U.S. 616 (1919), makes no mention of the "clear and present danger" doctrine there urged. It is interesting to compare Holmes's attitude toward legislative power in this case with that expressed by him in the Lochner case. What he criticized Justice Peckham for doing for "freedom of contract" in the latter case, he himself does for "freedom of speech" in the Abrams case. See p. 151 *supra*. The first case in which the Court definitely accepted the doctrine is Herndon *v.* Lowry, 301 U.S. 242, at 258 (1937).

extension became, indeed, a logical imperative when once it was recognized, as long ago it was, that liberty is something more than exemption from physical restraint, and that even in the field of substantive rights and duties the legislative judgment, if oppressive and arbitrary, may be overridden by the courts." [64]

Touching on the same subject a few months later, Chief Justice Stone suggested that "There may be narrower scope for operation of the presumption of constitutionality when legislation appears on its face to be within a specific prohibition of the Constitution, such as those of the first ten amendments, which are deemed equally specific when held to be embraced within the Fourteenth." And again: "It is unnecessary to consider now whether legislation which restricts those political processes which can ordinarily be expected to bring about repeal of undesirable legislation, is to be subjected to more exacting judicial scrutiny under the general prohibitions of the Fourteenth Amendment than are most other types of legislation." How the Chief Justice himself would have answered this question had he deemed it necessary to consider it is reasonably clear.[65]

[64] Palko v. Conn., 302 U.S. 319, at 327.

[65] United States v. Carolene Products Co., 304 U.S. 144, at 152–53, note 4 (1938). While the courts have from an early date taken a hand in crystallizing American conceptions of freedom of speech and press into law, it is scarcely in the manner or to the extent which they are frequently assumed to have done. The great initial problem in this realm of constitutional liberty was to get rid of the common law of "seditious libel" which operated to put persons in authority beyond the reach of public criticism. The first step in this direction was taken in the famous, or infamous, Sedition Act of 1798, which admitted the defense of truth in prosecutions brought under it, and submitted the general issue of defendant's guilt to the jury. But the substantive doc-

Meanwhile, between 1929 and 1937 had occurred the Great Depression, the most disruptive period in the history of American constitutional interpretation. The change which the views of a dominant section of the American people underwent during this period regarding the function of government in the economic field was

trine of "seditious libel" the Act of 1798 still retained, a circumstance which put several critics of President Adams in jail, and thereby considerably aided Jefferson's election as President in 1800. Once in office, nevertheless, Jefferson himself appealed to the discredited principle against partisan critics. Writing his friend Governor McKean of Pennsylvania in 1803 anent such critics, Jefferson said: "The federalists having failed in destroying the freedom of the press by their gag-law, seem to have attacked it in an opposite direction; that is by pushing its licentiousness and its lying to such a degree of prostitution as to deprive it of all credit. . . . This is a dangerous state of things, and the press ought to be restored to its credibility if possible. The restraints provided by the laws of the States are sufficient for this, if applied. And I have, therefore, long thought that a few prosecutions of the most prominent offenders would have a wholesome effect in restoring the integrity of the presses. Not a general prosecution, for that would look like persecution; but a selected one." *Works* (Ford ed., 1905), IX, 451-52.

In the *Memorial Edition* of Jefferson's works this letter is not included; nor apparently was it known to the Honorable Josephus Daniels, whose enthusiastic introduction to one of these volumes makes Jefferson out to have been the father of freedom of speech and press in this country, if not throughout the world. The sober truth is that it was that archenemy of Jefferson and of democracy, Alexander Hamilton, who made the greatest single contribution toward rescuing this particular freedom as a political weapon from the coils and toils of the common law, and that in connection with one of Jefferson's "selected prosecutions." I refer to Hamilton's many-times quoted formula in the Croswell case in 1804: "The liberty of the press is the right to publish with impunity, truth, with good motives, for justifiable ends though reflecting on government, magistracy, or individuals." People v. Croswell, 3 Johns (N.Y.) 337. Equipped with this brocard our State courts, working in co-operation with juries, whose attitude usually reflected the robustiousness of American political discussion before the

nothing short of revolutionary. Government helps those who help themselves was, roughly, the doctrine of *laissez faire;* it is peculiarly the duty of government to help those who are unable to help themselves was, roughly, the gospel of the New Deal. And from this major premise have issued certain corollaries which, as translated into terms of constitutional law, have compelled a radical recasting of some of its most fundamental doctrines.[66] In these pages, adhering to the pattern of the present chapter, I shall treat of this transvaluation of constitutional values only as it is reflected in the Court's more recent interpretation of the "due process" clauses of the Fifth and Fourteenth Amendments and especially in its current conceptions of "liberty."

The capitulation of the Court to the New Deal was somewhat uncertainly signalized in its decision of March 29, 1937, in West Coast Hotel Co. *v.* Parrish,[67] in which, overruling the District of Columbia Minimum Wage decision of 1923, it sustained, by a vote of 5 to 4, a minimum-wage law of the State of Washington. Inasmuch as the Court took "judicial notice of the existence of demands for relief occasioned by economic depression," it would seem that the overruling of the earlier case was not strictly necessary, since even in the District Minimum

---

Civil War, gradually wrote into the common law of the States the principle of "qualified privilege," which is a notification to plaintiffs in libel suits that if they are unlucky enough to be officeholders or office seekers, they must be prepared to shoulder the almost impossible burden of showing defendant's "special malice." Cooley, *Constitutional Limitations,* Chap. XII; Samuel A. Dawson, *Freedom of the Press, A Study of the Doctrine of "Qualified Privilege"* (Columbia Univ. Press, 1924).

[66] See Edward S. Corwin, *Constitutional Revolution, Ltd.* (2d ed.; Claremont Colleges, 1946).   [67] 300 U.S. 379.

Wage case it was conceded that the police power might in times of special emergency assume wider range.

The import of the Court's decision two weeks later in National Labor Relations Board *v.* Jones and Laughlin Corp.[68] was, however, unmistakable. Here the Court, again by a vote of 5 to 4, upheld the power of Congress to compel employers to permit their employees to organize and to bargain with them collectively, when to refuse to do so threatened to lead to strikes that would be crippling to interstate commerce. The company's argument that the act deprived them of freedom of contract and so of "liberty" without "due process of law" Chief Justice Hughes brushed aside with the assertion that "the right of employees to self-organization and to select representatives of their own choosing for collective bargaining . . . without restraint or coercion by their employer is a fundamental right," interference with which "is a proper subject for condemnation by competent legislative authority." He then continued: "Long ago we stated the reason for labor organizations. We said that they were organized out of the necessities of the situation; that a single employee was helpless in dealing with an employer; that he was dependent ordinarily on his daily wage for the maintenance of himself and family; and that if the employer refused to pay him the wages that he thought fair, he was nevertheless unable to leave the employ and resist arbitrary and unfair treatment; that union was essential to give laborers opportunity to deal on an equality with their employer." [69]

The significance of these words is twofold. In the first place, the Court definitely and decisively subordinates its

[68] 301 U.S. 1.   [69] *Ibid.,* 33.

previous conception of "liberty" as primarily freedom of contract to another type of "liberty" of which laborers are the beneficiaries. In the second place, "liberty" is recognized as something that may be infringed by other forces as well as by government; indeed, something that may require the positive intervention of government against these other forces. *From being a limitation on legislative power, the "due process" clause becomes an actual instigation to legislative action of a leveling character.* "Constitutional liberty" tends to be replaced by "civil liberty," as this term was defined in Chapter I.

In dealing with State legislation restrictive of the activities of labor the Court has, on the other hand, fallen back again on the "due process" clause of the Fourteenth Amendment, and with notable results. In this connection, two cases are of outstanding importance, Thornhill *v.* Alabama, decided in 1940, and American Federation of Labor *v.* Swing, decided in 1941.[70] In the former the Court, speaking by Justice Murphy, set aside an Alabama statute which, as applied by the courts of that State, forbade the peaceful picketing of the premises of anyone engaged in a lawful business. "In the circumstances of our times," said the Justice, "the dissemination of information concerning the facts of a labor dispute must be regarded as within the area of free discussion that is guaranteed by the Constitution." In the Swing case the same doctrine was applied against an injunction by the courts of Illinois which was based on *a rule of common law* of the State "forbidding resort to peaceful persuasion through picketing" when there was no immediate employer-employee relationship. The case logically implies that the

[70] 310 U.S. 88; 312 U.S. 321.

Supreme Court will undertake, as opportunity offers, to recast the common law of the several States defining the purposes for which laborers may strike without incurring the danger of being charged with "conspiracy."

In affixing the "freedom of speech" label to picketing, the Court has given it not only a new application but a new extension. As Justice Douglas, a thoroughgoing champion of recent developments, remarked in an opinion written in 1942, "Picketing by an organized group is more than free speech, since it involves patrol of a particular locality and since the very presence of a picket line may induce action of one kind or another, quite irrespective of the nature of the ideas which are being disseminated." [71] Furthermore, the picketer's audience is frequently an importuned one; and when it is, the picketer's right is an interference with the right of other people, not a complement thereof, as is the right of persons addressing those who come to hear them. Whether the doctrine of "clear and present danger" applies to legislative regulation of picketing the Court has had, apparently, no occasion thus far to say, but there seems to be no logical reason why it should not.

And the results it has reached in the effort to define the rights of organized labor the Court has employed simultaneously in interpretation of "religious liberty," with the result of giving it too a new dimension. The leading case is Cantwell v. Connecticut [72] in which the Court set aside the conviction of some Jehovah's Witnesses for soliciting funds in the public highways without a license, contrary to a State statute. In this case religious liberty was asserted to have *two* aspects: first, the right not to be

[71] 315 U.S. at 776 (1942).   [72] 310 U.S. 296 (1940).

compelled to accept a given creed or form of worship; secondly, the right to exercise freely one's chosen religion. Actually, the case involved a *third* aspect, the right to proselytize, and three years later in another Witnesses case the Court, speaking by Justice Douglas, acknowledged this to be the fact in the following words: "The hand distribution of religious tracts is an age-old form of missionary evangelism—as old as the printing presses. It has been a potent force in various religious movements down through the years. This form of evangelism is utilized today on a large scale by various religious sects whose colporteurs carry the Gospel to thousands upon thousands of homes and seek through personal visitations to win adherents to their faith. It is more than preaching; it is more than distribution of religious literature. It is a combination of both. Its purpose is as evangelical as the revival meeting. This form of religious activity occupies the same high estate under the First Amendment as do worship in the churches and preaching from the pulpits. It has the same claim to protection as the more orthodox and conventional exercises of religion. It also has the same claim as the others to the guarantees of freedom of speech and freedom of the press." [73] This unquestionably novel doctrine is not without its obvious practical difficulties. As Justice Jackson suggested in a dissenting opinion, the Court ought to ask itself what would be the effect "if the right given these Witnesses should be exercised by all sects and denominations." [74]

[73] 319 U.S. at 109 (1943).
[74] Religious liberty seems to have called forth very few judicial utterances against repressive legislation prior to the Civil War. *Ex parte* Newman, 9 Calif. 502 (1858) was one exception to the rule. The act

But the Cantwell case is notable also as being the first in a series of three cases in which the Court has, after much vacillation, discarded the doctrine of presumed constitutionality for State action designed to elicit "affirma-

---

involved was a Sabbath observance law. The petitioner is described as "an Israelite, engaged in the business of selling clothing at Sacramento" and his offense as "the sale of goods on Sunday." The act was set aside as violative of the State constitution. Said Chief Justice Terry: "While we concede to the Legislature all the supremacy to which it is entitled, we cannot yield to it the omnipotence which has been ascribed to the British Parliament, so long as we have a Constitution which limits its powers, and places certain innate rights of the citizen beyond its control. . . .

"It is the settled doctrine of this court to enforce every provision of the Constitution in favor of the rights reserved to the citizen against a usurpation of power in any question whatsoever; and although in a doubtful case we would yield to the authority of the Legislature, yet upon the question before us, we are constrained to declare that, in our opinion, the act in question is in conflict with the first section of article first of the Constitution, because, without necessity, it infringes upon the liberty of the citizen, by restraining his right to acquire property.

"And that it is in conflict with the fourth section of the same article, because it was intended as, and is in effect, a discrimination in favor of one religious profession, and gives it a preference over all others.

"It follows that the prisoner was improperly convicted, and it is ordered that he be discharged from custody."

Justice Burnett added: "The right to protect and possess property is not more clearly protected by the Constitution than the right to acquire. The right to acquire must include the right to use the proper means to attain the end. The right itself would be impotent without the power to use its necessary incidents. The Legislature, therefore, cannot prohibit the proper use of the means of acquiring property, except the peace and safety of the State require it. . . ." This stress on the right to acquire property tends to assimilate the decision to the contemporary doctrine of vested rights, and makes the more curious Justice Stephen Field's dissent. Later, when he became Chief Justice, Field succeeded in getting the Court to overrule its previous decision. *Ex parte* Andrews, 18 Calif. 685. Not long afterward he was appointed to the United States Supreme Court, where, as we have seen, he became the spokesman par excellence of laissez-faire individualism.

tion of a belief or attitude of mind." In the Cantwell case itself the State set aside a conviction for the common-law offense of breach of the peace in a situation in which the "clear and present danger" rule was pressed to the extreme. Yet, a fortnight later, the same Court all but unanimously sustained a Pennsylvania school board in excluding from the public schools children of Jehovah's Witnesses who, for professedly religious motives, had refused to salute the flag.[75] This time the Court put its reliance on the doctrine of presumed constitutionality. Then three years later this precedent too went into the discard, thanks to the conversion meantime of an all but unanimous Court to the view of the dissenters in the Pennsylvania case. This occurred in West Virginia State Board of Education v. Barnette,[76] in which a West Virginia flag-salute law was held void as to unwilling compliants.

Said Justice Jackson for the Court, "It is now a commonplace that censorship or suppression of expression of opinion is tolerated by our Constitution only when the expression presents a clear and present danger of action of a kind the State is empowered to prevent and punish. It would seem that involuntary affirmation could be commanded only on even more immediate and urgent grounds than silence. . . . To sustain the compulsory flag salute we are required to say that a Bill of Rights which guards the individual's right to speak his own mind, left it open to public authorities to compel him to utter what is not in his mind." [77]

Furthermore, as Justice Jackson takes pains to an-

---

[75] Minersville School Dist. v. Gobitis, 310 U.S. 586 (1940).
[76] 319 U.S. 624 (1943); see also Taylor v. Miss., 319 U.S. 583.
[77] *Ibid.*, at pp. 633–34.

nounce, the doctrine of the case is intended to cover all areas of belief, secular as well as religious. "If," says he, "there is any fixed star in our constitutional constellation, it is that no official, high or petty, can prescribe what shall be orthodox in politics, nationalism, religion, or other matters of opinion or force citizens to confess by word or act their faith therein. If there are any circumstances which permit an exception, they do not now occur to us." [78] At the same time, he frankly owns that "the task of translating the majestic generalities of the Bill of Rights, conceived as part of the pattern of liberal government in the eighteenth century, into concrete restraints on officials dealing with the problems of the twentieth century, is one to disturb self-confidence. These principles," he continues, "grew in soil which also produced a philosophy that the individual was the center of society, that his liberty was attainable through mere absence of governmental restraints, and that government should be entrusted with few controls and only the mildest supervision over men's affairs. We must transplant these rights to a soil in which the laissez-faire concept or principle of non-interference has withered at least as to economic affairs, and social advancements are increasingly sought through closer integration of society and through expanded and strengthened governmental controls. These changed conditions often deprive precedents of reliability and cast us more than we would choose upon our own judgment. But we [the Court] act in these matters not by authority of our competence but by force of our commissions. We cannot, because of modest estimates of our competence in such specialties as public edu-

[78] *Ibid.*, at p. 642.

cation, withhold the judgment that history authenticates as the function of this Court when liberty is infringed." [79] Read in the light of more recent events, these words do not exaggerate the difficulties of the Court's role as the champion of freedom of opinion.

One other phase of recent interpretation of the "due process" clause of the Fourteenth Amendment may be dealt with more briefly. It represents nothing less than the revival and reanimation, so to speak, of the clause in its pristine procedural sense. In Hurtado v. California,[80] the Court, stating that there is no superfluous language in the Constitution, took the position that while the "due process" clause of the Fourteenth Amendment required that criminal trials be "fair," it did not lay upon the States the same procedural requirements that are stipulated in the Fifth and Sixth Amendments for trials in the national courts. When, however, the Court, following World War I, began defining the word "liberty" in the amendment by reading into it the restrictions which the First Amendment imposes upon Congress, this line of reasoning was rendered obsolete, and since then the Court has supervised with increasing diligence trial procedures in the States, particularly in those cases in which conviction is accompanied by denial of counsel to defendant, or is alleged to be based on coerced confessions, or in which discrimination has been shown in the selection of juries and grand juries.[81]

Recent interpretation of the Fourteenth Amendment reveals, therefore, a distinctly equalitarian slant. This ap-

[79] Ibid., at pp. 639–40.   [80] See pp. 134–36 supra.
[81] Powell v. Ala., 287 U.S. 45 (1932); Chambers v. Fla., 309 U.S. 227 (1940); Patton v. Miss., decided December 15, 1947.

pears in the encouragement which it lends to reformist legislation, and especially to legislation meant to augment the bargaining power of labor. It appears in the types of human activity which it supports against restrictive legislation, that of aggressive labor groups and of proselytizing religious sects. It appears again in the restored usefulness of the "due process" clause as a gauge of fair procedure in behalf of accused persons, since most of the cases raising this issue have come up from the South and have been infused with the racial tensions of that part of the country. It appears, finally, in the Court's partial reanimation recently of Congress' powers under section 5 of the amendment.[82]

The Fourteenth Amendment may thus be restored in time to the use for which it was primarily intended when it was first adopted. Meantime, the "due process" clause thereof will have furnished the core of a vast body of jurisprudence much of which has within the last decade been consigned by the tribunal that elaborated it to the limbo of things outlived. Whether the same tribunal's recent doctrines will prove more viable in the long run only the long run can tell. Some of them appear likely to undergo sharp challenge in no remote future.[83]

[82] Screws v. U.S., 325 U.S. 91 (1945); Julius Cohen, "The Screws Case, Federal Protection of Negro Rights," 46 *Columbia Law Review,* 94–106 (1946).

[83] See Appendix II for further discussion of certain topics which have a collateral bearing on the main theme of this chapter.

CHAPTER V

RÉSUMÉ AND CRITIQUE

We have been tracing the story of an idea. From Cicero to the latest decision of the Supreme Court stretches a continuous tradition of two thousand years which asserts that there are rights made of no human hands and beyond the rightful reach of human hands. With Cicero himself the idea of Liberty against Government is incidental to the broader conception of a universal justice which ought to animate all human legislation and pervade all acts of human authority. But 1,200 years later the narrower idea of a recourse *against* authority becomes, in John Salisbury's *Policraticus*, the significant core of a gospel which Bracton summed up in the thirteenth century in the famous brocard, "The King ought to be under no man, but under God and the law (*sub deo et lege*)." And meantime in Magna Carta, in Bracton's words "*constitutio libertatis*," this idea had found documentary embodiment. Under the later Plantagenet and the early Lancastrian monarchs Magna Carta took on the semblance of a written constitution even as we know such instruments. By command of the English monarch, both his own further orders and those of his officers contrary to the Char-

ter were to be disregarded, and by the requirement of
Parliament any of its own statutes contrary to the Charter were to be "held for null."

Later, it is true, the Charter recedes into the background, being replaced by and absorbed into the law of
the courts, the common law. In Sir John Fortescue's pages,
In Praise of the Law of England (*De Laudibus Legum
Angliae*), the common law is at once a "law of liberty"
and the peculiar property, the craft mystery, of Bench
and Bar. Indeed, but for the corporate solidarity of the
English Bench and Bar, centering in the Inns of Court,
the conception of a "higher law" of liberty would in all
probability have been lost to the England from whose institutions the American constitutional tradition takes its
rise. In accomplishing through their Parliaments the ecclesiastical revolution of England, the Tudors restored to
the world the notion of an unlimited lawmaking authority
anchored in the popular will—an idea which had been
illustrated two thousand years before in the popular assemblies of ancient Greece and Rome.

Fortunately for the survival of the idea of a higher law
of liberty, the Stuart kings endeavored early in the seventeenth century, just as the first English settlers were land-
ing on American shores, to capture for themselves the
ultimate power in the English realm. The result was a re-
action, headed by Sir Edward Coke, to the constitutional
ideas of Plantagenet and Lancastrian England. Initially,
as Chief Justice, Coke thought to claim for the ordinary
courts the power to adjudicate between King and Parliament and in this persuasion he laid in Bonham's Case the
foundations of the instrument of judicial review, destined
to become two hundred years later the citadel of Ameri-

can constitutionalism. Forced subsequently to abandon this ambitious enterprise, Coke thrust forward "The High Court of Parliament" as the final interpretive agency of a Fundamental Law which bound both the monarch and itself, and of which Magna Carta was the supreme embodiment.

Coke's teaching, however, did not escape the defects of its qualities. As the sage of the common law, he extolled its claims, as had Fortescue before him, as a craft mystery, but reversing Fortescue, who had infused the common law with the still-vital spirit of Magna Carta, Coke poured into the revived and reanimated Charter the spirit of the matured common law. In consequence, his higher law of liberty became contracted for the most part to the ancient procedures of that same law. So, when our ancestors launched the agitation which led to the Declaration of Independence, they found Coke's conception of an English constitution, restrictive even of the powers of Parliament, inadequate for their purposes. Indeed, before the quarrel reached its culmination Coke had been largely superseded as the oracle of the English constitution by Blackstone, who found in the sovereignty of Parliament the main pillar of that constitution.

To whom then were the colonists to appeal for justification for taking up arms against King and Parliament? The answer was supplied by John Locke's second *Treatise on Civil Government*, which had been written to justify the Glorious Revolution of 1688. Locke goes straight back to the Ciceronian conception of a law of nature, which he purges of its medieval and theological trappings, and then transmutes through the dissolving agency of the social compact into a higher law of the inalienable rights of the individual. Government rests with Locke on the consent of the governed, but this consent is a conditioned one, since no man is competent to contract for the establishment over himself of arbitrary power. Locke thus replaces Coke's insistence on the historic procedures of the common law with emphasis on the substantive rights which these procedures were designed to protect, and which he sums up with the designation of "Property." He is careful to explain that he is using the term in a broad sense, but in the history of American constitutional law his nomenclature, reflective of the common law, originally proved more influential than his professed intention.

The blended traditions of Coke and Locke were conveyed into the incipient stream of American constitutional law by the bills of rights of the early State constitutions and by judicial review, which soon after 1800 became a feature of all of them. For most private rights the former, supported by the representative character of American institutions, have generally proved sufficient, but for one class of rights, those associated with ownership, such, it was discovered very early, was not the case. Owing to the persistence of the notion that they were the American equivalents of the British Parliament, the early State legislatures interfered at will with judicial decisions affecting vested rights, while in the nature of things the interests most immediately and most detrimentally affected by reform legislation were generally the proprietarian. The unfavorable situation of property was countered in the first instance by the State courts, when, with the encouragement of the Supreme Court, they reverted to the type of judicial review which was suggested by Bonham's Case, one based on extraconstitutional principles. And the grand result of this species of judicial activity, in which Bench and Bar co-operated, was the *doctrine of vested rights,* which erected as the primary test of legislation its effect on existing property rights and classified as punitive and hence unconstitutional any legislation which bore with undue harshness on such rights. As systematized by Kent in his famous *Commentaries,* the doctrine eventually watered down all the powers of the State—those of taxation, of eminent domain, and of "regulation," which Kent sharply distinguished from the power of uncompensated "destruction."

The doctrine of vested rights attained its meridian in the early thirties, when it came under attack from two sources. The first of these was the notion that the written constitution, being an expression of popular will, was the supreme law of the State and that judicial review could validly operate only on that basis; the second was the related idea, which is connoted by the term "police power"—that legislation which was not specifically forbidden by the written constitution must be presumed to have been enacted in the *public interest.* Confronted with these doctrines, the champions of the doctrine of vested rights were compelled to find some clause of the written constitution which could be thrown about the doctrine or else to abandon it.

Again the ingenuity of Bench and Bar were equal to the exigency. Most State constitutions contained from the outset a paraphrase of chapter 29 of Magna Carta, which declared that no person should be deprived of his "estate" "except by the law of the land or a judgment of his peers"; and following the usage of the Fifth Amend-

ment of the United States Constitution, more and more
State constitutions came after 1791 to contain a clause
which, paraphrasing a statute of Plantagenet times, declared that "no person shall be deprived of life, liberty
or property without due process of law." By the outbreak
of the Civil War a more or less complete transference of
the doctrine of vested rights and most of its Kentian corollaries had been effected in the vast majority of the State
jurisdictions. One exception was Kent's distinction between the power of "regulation," which he conceded the
State, and that of "destruction," which he denied it unless
it was prepared to compensate disadvantaged owners. The
division of judicial opinion on this point was signalized
in the middle fifties, when the New York Court of Appeals, in the great Wynehamer case, stigmatized a State-
wide prohibition statute as an act of destruction, in its
application to existing stocks of liquor, which was beyond
the power of the State legislature to authorize *even by
the procedures of due process of law.* In several other
States similar statutes were sustained in the name of the
"police power."

Did the doctrine of vested rights reflect a rift in the
American democracy between the American people in
general and the Bench and Bar, whose achievements the
initial establishment of the doctrine and its later transference within the ramparts of the written constitution
definitely were? Certainly not till recent times, and for
the reason that, as Charles Pinckney had put it in the
Philadelphia Convention, there was "more equality of
rank and fortune in America than in any country under
the sun," and that this was "likely to continue as long

as the unappropriated western lands remained unsettled." [1] So while De Tocqueville observed in 1834, when the doctrine of vested rights was at its height, that if he were asked where he placed the American aristocracy, he would "reply without hesitation, that it is not composed of the rich, who are united together by no common tie, but that it occupies the judicial bench and the bar," [2] he later added: "In no country in the World is the love of property more active and more anxious than in the United States; nowhere does the majority display less inclination for those principles which threaten to alter, in whatever manner, the laws of property." [3] The latter observation

[1] See Farrand (ed.), *Records*, I, 397–401 (Madison's *Notes* for June 25).

[2] *Democracy in America* (1873), I, 304.

[3] *Ibid.*, II, 272. It is pertinent to notice, too, that De Tocqueville's chief fear for the continuance of free institutions in the United States arose from the equality of conditions among the Americans and their overweening attachment to sentiments of equality and contempt for pretensions of superiority. *Ibid.*, 102, 306–307, 323, 343. A German contemporary of De Tocqueville, on the other hand, Professor Robert von Mohl of Tübingen, fixing his attention upon American constitutional arrangements, felt that the Americans had found answers for two of the greatest problems that could arise in the political field. Reviewing Story's *Commentaries* the same year that De Tocqueville began bringing out in Paris his *De la Democratie en Amerique*, von Mohl wrote: "The institutions of the Union are highly interesting, in having solved, in a perfectly satisfactory manner, the double problem, 1st, the establishment of a democracy in a territory of great extent; and 2ndly, the reconciling of the necessary participation of all the citizens in the conducting of public affairs, with the modern passive notions of freedom, to wit, with the requirement that the pursuit of private purposes shall be as little as possible impeded or interfered with by the State:—two problems, the solution of which, at first view, seem impossible." Democracy and *laissez faire* were not incompatible, in short. Von Mohl, however, criticizes Story for not including an account of

is, moreover, confirmed by the fact that, far from manifesting any desire to curb judicial review in favor of the property right, the American States have continued even to this day to incorporate in their constitutions those provisions on which the security of property against legislative majorities came ultimately to rest. Partly, no doubt, this was the inertia of custom and habit; but it is none the less significant that till recently the habit was never seriously challenged.

The adoption of the Fourteenth Amendment in 1868 provided the framework for the reception by the Supreme Court of the United States of the results which had been reached in the State jurisdictions in adjudicating the conflicting claims of the property right and the police power. But the amendment went much farther than this; for in forbidding State legislation which abridged "privileges and immunities of citizens of the United States" it laid a sufficient foundation for the protection by the Court of all the fundamental rights of citizenship under a free government; and while it was the plight of the freedmen which evoked the amendment in the first instance, yet its indicated beneficiaries were all American citizens, regardless of race or color. These resplendent possibilities of the amendment for the cause of Liberty against Government were not realized, however, for several reasons.

To begin with, the dominant majority of the Court

American administrative law in his work; and comments unfavorably on the inability that Americans are under to bring suit against their governments without the consent of the latter. 14 *American Jurist* (1835), 330 ff. Von Mohl's familiarity with American federalism is fully attested by his *Das Bundes-Staatsrecht der Vereinigten Staaten von Nord-Amerika* (Stuttgart, 1824).

for several years following the adoption of the amendment comprised members whose interest in constitutional
interpretation was derived from pre-Civil War days and
hence focussed on the issue of States' Rights against National Power. To their way of thinking, the power vested
in Congress by the fifth section of the amendment to enforce its other provisions by "appropriate legislation" con-
stituted a serious menace to the "federal equilibrium," and
one which would be augmented in proportion as the
Court took a broad view of its own powers under the first
section. So in 1873, in the famous Slaughter House Cases,
the Court simply drew a blue pencil through the "privileges and immunities" clause, at the same time disavowing largely any ambition on its own part to become "a
perpetual censor on all State legislation" affecting civil
rights.

This self-denying ordinance left the "due process"
clause of section 1 still standing, nevertheless; and in their
dissents in the Slaughter House Cases, Justices Bradley and
Swayne affixed to the words "liberty" and "property" a
construction which was capable of filling a great part of
the gap created by the obliteration of the "privileges and
immunities" clause. Naturally the majority of the Court
rejected these expansive views too, and were, moreover,
supported by Cooley's recently published *Constitutional
Limitations* in doing so. While confessing his bias in favor
of laissez-faire concepts, Cooley in his capacity as commentator nevertheless scrupulously stopped short initially
in his exposition of "law of the land" and "due process of
law" with an endorsement of the decision of the New
York Court of Appeals in the Wynehamer case.

Not till a full decade later was the Court able to cut

the tie which had hitherto bound its own fortunes to those of Congress in relation to the Fourteenth Amendment. This it did in the Civil Rights Cases of 1883, in which it disallowed the Civil Rights Act of 1875 on the basis of the proposition that Congress' power under section 5 was only the power to disallow *positive* State action hostile to the provisions of section 1—a power not substantially greater than the much more readily applicable power of judicial review of the Court itself.

And with the danger to the federal equilibrium from Congressional legislation under section 5 thus removed, or at least materially reduced, the Court might now, it would seem, have begun to reappraise its own powers under section 1 in a more liberal spirit. Indeed, in the Hurtado case, which followed the Civil Rights Cases by a few months, just such a development was apparently forecast in Justice Matthews' opinion for the Court. Not only was the Court empowered, said he, it was indeed obligated, by the "due process" clause of the Fourteenth Amendment to disallow all "arbitrary" State action of whatever character, executive, legislative, or judicial.

Except in the field of rate regulation, the prediction, or promise, turned out to be premature. The decision in the Slaughter House Cases still stood, fortified indeed by a half-dozen reiterations; and the implied ban of Cooley's authoritative pages on expansive ideas of "liberty" still stood, and meantime a new difficulty had emerged. In Munn *v.* Illinois the Court was brought to realize clearly for the first time that when it was called upon to adjudicate between the police power and the property right under the "due process" clause, it was confronted with what in the last analysis was a question of fact. Did facts exist to justify the challenged enactment or not? In the Munn case the Court, answering this question in harmony with the doctrine that a State statute must be presumed to be constitutional till clearly shown to be otherwise, laid down the rule that "if a state of facts could exist that would justify such legislation," "we must assume" that "it actually did exist when the statute under consideration was passed." So long as this formula was adhered to it presented a stone wall against which, as statistics show, lawyers and clients were not anxious to break their heads.[4]

The final acceptance by the Court of an enlarged power of judicial review under the "due process" clause of the Fourteenth Amendment was the outcome of a systematic effort on the part of leaders of the American Bar at self-indoctrination in the gospel of *laissez faire,* for which Bradley's definition of "liberty" in his Slaughter House opinion was found to supply an apt translation into the terminology of constitutional law. The effort began with the foundation of the American Bar Association in 1878. The leading State courts began to succumb to it in 1885. Yet not till nearly thirty years after the adoption of the amendment did the Supreme Court formally ratify the Bradley doctrine, which it at the same time trimmed down to the doctrine of freedom of contract in the field of industrial relations. The Peckham opinion in the Lochner case, decided in 1905 is the classic statement of the judicial version of laissez-faireism. It boils down to the direct reversal of the rule of presumed constitutionality in the case of State legislation regulating the conditions

[4] See especially Appendix E in Charles W. Collins, *The Fourteenth Amendment and the States* (1912).

of labor of mature workers in the ordinary employments. The methodology and the ideology of the Lochner decision, although departed from at times in the interval between, were still those of the Court on the eve of the New Deal constitutional revolution.

The counterpart of the question raised above as to the accordance of the doctrine of vested rights with American democratic beliefs arises as regards the doctrine of freedom of contract. Certainly the two doctrines, especially when they are projected against the social environments in which they respectively arose, are two quite different things. Ownership as a source of private and family well-being is one thing; ownership as a source of control over others is another thing; and as the prerogative of great corporations dealing with unorganized workingmen, ownership—ordinarily an absentee ownership—is obviously of the latter description. Moreover, while corporate ownership was expanding, opportunities for personal acquisition were contracting.

Exactly fifty years after De Tocqueville began publishing his *Democracy in America*, a British observer, Sir Henry Maine, recorded his impression of the American scene in the following words: "There has hardly ever before been a community in which the weak have been pushed so pitilessly to the wall, in which those who have succeeded have so uniformly been the strong, and in which in so short a time there has arisen so great an inequality of private fortune and domestic luxury. And at the same time, there has never been a country in which, on the whole, the persons distanced in the race have suffered so little from their ill-success. All this beneficent prosperity is the fruit of recognizing the principle of population, and the one remedy for its excess in perpetual emigration. It all reposes on the sacredness of contract and the stability of private property, the first the implement, and the last the reward, of success in the universal competition." [5]

But by the middle eighties the possibility of "perpetual emigration" was virtually at an end. Yet not for another decade and more did the Court incorporate the doctrine of freedom of contract in its interpretation of the Fourteenth Amendment. The doctrine had meantime become an anachronism.

The way was in some measure made smooth for the recent constitutional revolution when following World War I the Court, repudiating a rule of construction of the "due process" clause of the Fourteenth Amendment which it had followed for more than forty years, announced its acceptance of the thesis that the "liberty" there mentioned included freedom of speech and press, a concession which was later amplified by its ratification of the "clear and present danger" rule. The matrix of the revolution itself was the conviction borne in upon the American people as a whole by the Great Depression that government must intervene in the economic field when private ownership and management fail to provide living conditions for any considerable section of the population. The two important results for constitutional interpretation of the revolution so far have been the subordination in the scale of constitutional values protected by the "due process" clause, of freedom of contract of employers to the right of their employees to organize and bargain collectively and the classification of the right

[5] Sir Henry Maine, *Popular Government* (London, 1885), 51.

of strikers to picket peaceably as "freedom of speech."
Contemporaneously, the Court has manifested a new
hospitality, possibly overdone at times, to the claims on
it of proselytizing religious minorities, and a new alert-
ness to the similar claims of racial minorities.

In short, the term "liberty" has left behind the purely
proprietarian connotations it inherited from the doctrine
of vested rights, and in so doing it has taken on a distinctly equalitarian tinge. Nor is there anything excep-
tionable in this in itself. In the Ciceronian-Lockian conception of natural law, liberty and equality are not hostile,
but friendly conceptions; and in the Declaration of Independence the same amicable relationship holds: "All men
are created equal and are endowed by their Creator with
certain unalienable rights." In the legalistic tradition, on
which judicial review has operated in the past for the most
part, "liberty" and "equality" are, on the other hand, apt
to appear as opposed values, the former as the peculiar
care of the courts, the latter the peculiar care of the legislature. It is easy to imagine in the light shed by current
ideologies that the demands upon the legislative power,
national and State, might so multiply in behalf of "the
common man," whose century this is said to be, that the
notion of Liberty against Government and its implement, judicial review, would be gradually but inexorably
crowded to the wall.

Perhaps it is true of the social as of the inanimate
world, that a sort of Second Law of Thermodynamics
holds sway, so that the energies of the mass of men tend
to a common level of achievement and of hoped for
security; perhaps, indeed, that is what is meant when it
is said that this is "the century of the common man." The

great question is, can the "common man," unaided by the uncommon man, keep civilization going—will he wish to make the effort? This question, fortunately, does not exhaust the possibilities. For it is possible that the uncommon man will seek to achieve self-realization less and less in terms of self-advancement and self-exploitation, more and more in terms of co-operative endeavor and community advantage.

Certain it is that signs multiply about us daily to affirm the prophetic vision of the words with which more than a century ago De Tocqueville concluded his great work: "The nations of our time cannot prevent the conditions of men from becoming equal; but it depends upon themselves whether the principle of equality is to lead them to servitude or freedom, to knowledge or barbarism, to prosperity or to wretchedness."

APPENDIX I

A BOOK REVIEW *

CONSTITUTIONALISM: ANCIENT AND MODERN.
By Charles Howard McIlwain. Ithaca: Cornell University Press, 1940. Pp. ix, 162;
CONSTITUTIONALISM AND THE CHANGING
WORLD. By Charles Howard McIlwain. New York:
The Macmillan Company, 1939. Pp. viii, 313.

The first of these volumes, a revision of six lectures which
Professor McIlwain delivered at Cornell University in the
academic year 1938–39, is an outgrowth of the author's previous studies in the fields of political theory and constitutional history, but it is in no sense a summary or condensation
of these studies. It adds to them, and the fresh contribution
which it makes is one of great significance not only to
scholarship, but to an understanding of issues which threaten
to shatter our contemporary civilization. The theme of the
work is the rise of the idea of Limited Government, and at
a time when "faiths and empires gleam like wrecks of a dissolving dream," it points to the deeply laid foundations of
this conception in English medieval institutions and legal
ideas.

The beginning of the story, to be sure, reaches much

* 54 *Harvard Law Review*, 533–35 (January, 1941).

further back. Indeed, it seems to me that Professor McIlwain wastes some valuable time and precious space in a rather fruitless effort to demonstrate that "there is little comfort to be derived from" Plato "by believers in totalitarianism" (p. 37). No convinced Nazi could ever be unconvinced that Hitler has not, in the words of the *Politicus*, shown "a strength of art which is superior to law" (p. 34). The real fountain-head of the tradition here traced is a twofold one, the Stoic conception of a law of nature anterior to all human authority and the Roman conception of *lex* as resting ultimately on the consent of the whole people. Building on these foundations, Cicero defined the state "as a bond of law (*vinculum juris*)" (p. 39), and added that "no state can ever enact binding law in derogation" of the law of nature (p. 40). True, the idea that popular consent lay at the basis of all authority came ultimately to be invoked as the source and justification of imperial absolutism, as in the famous text of the *Institutes*, "*Quod principi placuit legis habet vigorem, cum lege regia . . . populus ei et in eum omne suum imperium et potestatem conferat.*" Even so, in being thus invoked, the idea that "none but the whole *populus* can be the ultimate source of legal authority" was given enduring expression; and Professor McIlwain advances what he terms "the de-batable . . . but defensible" thesis that "the really decisive influence of Rome on later European politics came, not after the Italian Renaissance in the tendency toward absolutism, but during the Middle Ages in the reinforcement of con-stitutionalism" (pp. 59–60).

Certain it is that the outstanding contribution of the volume is to be found in its fourth chapter, which is entitled "Consti-tutionalism in the Middle Ages." Here the discussion centers about Bracton's great work, *De Legibus et Consuetudinibus Angliae*, which brought the barbaric chaos of the rising com-mon law under the civilizing influence of Roman legal rubrics and jurisprudential concepts. The riddle which Professor

McIlwain sets out to solve is the one offered by the conceded contradiction of certain passages of the *De Legibus* respecting the King's relation to the law. The most famous sentence of the *De Legibus* undoubtedly is that which proclaims that "the King himself ought not to be subject to man, but subject to God and the law, for the law makes the King" (f. 5b., Twiss ed.). Yet, almost in the same breath, Bracton quotes the *Digna vox* of the Emperors Theodosius and Valentinian to the effect that "it is a worthy voice of reigning majesty to profess that the prince is bound by the laws"—"which seems" as Professor McIlwain puts it, "properly to indicate nothing more than a check upon the prince's actions by himself alone and of his own free will" (p. 74). How is such a fundamental inconsistency to be explained?

One clue to an answer Professor McIlwain finds in Bracton's quotation of the maxim "*Quod principi*," etc., without the final verb "*conferat.*" The "*cum*," which in the original means "because," thus becomes "with," and the maxim comes to mean that the prince's will is law "together with the *lex regia* which has been laid down concerning his authority." And this statement Professor McIlwain interprets as signifying, in effect, that for the royal will to be law it must accord with the ancient customs as declared by the magnates of the realm (p. 73), and as sworn to in the royal coronation oath. "The King's coronation oath," he asserts, "is in fact Bracton's *lex regia*" (p. 74).

But a clue is one thing; solution is another. The solution which Professor McIlwain provides to "the riddle of Bracton"—"in reality the riddle of our medieval constitutionalism" (p. 76)—is "the clearcut separation which Bracton . . . makes between *gubernaculum* and *jurisdictio*—discretion and law—allowing the King an autocratic and irresponsible authority within the former, but never beyond it" (p. 81; see also pp. 79–80, 82, 87–89). This distinction, as Professor McIlwain points out, approximates that between government, in the narrower sense of administration, and law. It ripens in time into that between the prerogative and the realm of *meum* and *tuum* where the common law held sway; and it is reflected today in American constitutional law in the distinction between "political" and "justiciable" questions.

Yet, clear-cut as this distinction was in principle, the line between *gubernaculum* and *jurisdictio* often became blurred in practice for the simple reason that for centuries there was no continuously functioning agency capable of maintaining it against the unremitting attrition of royal pretensions. *Parliaments* there were, to be sure, but till 1689 no Parliament (pp. 109–10); and while the courts, even as early as Elizabeth's reign, occasionally asserted the power to "admeasure the prerogatives of the King" upon the law, both statute and common (pp. 116–17, 123), they too were an uncertain reliance (p. 128). In Ship-Money Case, to take a noteworthy instance, the judges defined the prerogative first, and then set it up as a limit to Parliament's power (p. 138). So when the dispute which led to the great Civil War arose, the King was able to back his pretensions with a host of precedents (*facta*) which his opponents were able to stigmatize, on the score of *doctrine*, as acts of sheer usurpation.

Such, in outline, is Professor McIlwain's major thesis. He brings to its support a wealth of materials and a cogency of reasoning of which it is impossible within the limitations of a review such as this to convey more than a hint. When, on the other hand, he seeks to bring the distinction between *gubernaculum* and *jurisdictio* to the clarification of current issues, I find him rather less persuasive. "The limiting of government," he contends, "is not the weakening of it" (p. 145); and on this premise he rejects "political balances" while extolling judicial review as a means of maintaining *jurisdictio* against the overweening claims of *gubernaculum* these days. This seems to me to attribute to judicial review an automatic quality which "our past constitutional history" (p. 147) does not confirm.

The second volume before us is especially welcome for rendering available between two covers the fifteen previously published essays and papers which it contains. Though drawn from a variety of sources, its contents reveal a central theme, and again it is Limited Government. In several of the papers, the particular aspect dealt with is the idea that "sovereignty" is historically a legal concept and implies legal limitation in its very statement. To be sure, the sovereign—Bodin's sovereign, for instance—is *legibus solutus* so far as concerns the laws which he makes, but he is not *legibus solutus* as respects the law which makes him sovereign and invests him with law-making power.

The two longest essays are entitled "Due Process of Law in Magna Carta" and "Magna Carta and Common Law." In the latter, it is shown how Magna Carta came gradually to be looked upon "as an enactment in affirmance of fundamental common law, to be confirmed and observed as a part of that law" (p. 176). In the former, an effort is made to identify this same fundamental common law, or the part of it which existed when Magna Carta was issued, with the *legem terrae* of the famous chapter 39 of that document. In other words, the effort is made to give these words a *substantive* content, whereas most previous writers had treated them as referring only to procedure. In an "Additional Note" Professor McIlwain abandons his reading in favor of one by Professor Radin, which revives the procedural sense of the term, but with a novel content.

Needless to say, we find in these pages the same wealth of learning, the same close reasoning, and the same power to invest the subject with interest which distinguish all Professor McIlwain's writings, and make them an unfailing source of intellectual stimulation to his readers.

Edward S. Corwin.

APPENDIX II

ADDENDUM TO
CHAPTER IV

In his opinion in the Slaughter House Cases, Justice Miller asserted that "the one pervading purpose" of the War Amendments was "the freedom of the slave race . . . and the protection of newly made freemen" in their rights as citizens; and in harmony with this position he dismissed argument for the plaintiffs based on the "equal protection" clause with the statement: "We doubt very much whether any action of a State not directed by way of discrimination against the negroes as a class, or on account of their race, will ever be held to come within the purview" of this clause. In these words the Court brushed aside Campbell's emphatic assertion for plaintiffs that protection of the freedmen was only incidental to a much broader purpose, that of giving constitutional embodiment to the principle of "laissez-faire individualism which had been held by the Colonists ever since they came to this soil." As is amply shown in Chapter IV of this work, Campbell proved in the long run much the better prophet, a fact which invites attention to the interesting episode in the judicial history of the Fourteenth Amendment, of which Howard Jay Graham writes in his article "The 'Conspiracy Theory' of the Fourteenth Amendment," *Selected Essays on Constitutional Law* (1938), I, 236–67.

"In an argument before the Supreme Court of the United States in 1882," Graham narrates, "Roscoe Conkling, a former member of the Joint Congressional Committee which in 1866 drafted the Fourteenth Amendment, produced for the first time the manuscript journal of the Committee, and by means of extensive quotations and pointed comment conveyed the impression that he and his colleagues in drafting the due process and equal protection clauses intentionally used the word 'person' in order to include corporations. 'At the time the Fourteenth Amendment was ratified,' he declared, 'individuals and joint stock companies were appealing for congressional and administrative protection against invidious and discriminating State and local taxes. One instance was that of an express company, whose stock was owned largely by citizens of the State of New York. . . .' The unmistakable inference was that the joint Committee had taken cognizance of these appeals and had drafted its text with particular regard for corporations.

"Coming from a man who had twice declined a seat on the Supreme Bench, who spoke from first hand knowledge, and who submitted a manuscript record in support of his stand, so dramatic an argument could not fail to make a profound impression. Within the next few years the Supreme Court began broadening its interpretation of the Fourteenth Amendment, and early in 1886 it unanimously affirmed Conkling's proposition, namely that corporations were 'persons' within the meaning of the equal protection clause. It is literally true therefore that Roscoe Conkling's argument sounded the death knell of the narrow 'Negro-race theory' of the Fourteenth Amendment expounded by Justice Miller in the Slaughter House cases. By doing this it cleared the way for the modern development of due process of law and the corresponding expansion of the Court's discretionary powers over social and economic legislation. Viewed in perspective, the argument is one of the landmarks in American constitutional history, an important turning point in our social and economic development."

Whether Conkling's argument is actually the landmark in American constitutional history that Graham asserts it was I shall consider later. At this point, I wish to summarize briefly his evaluation of the charge which certain historians began making after 1914, when the Journal used by Conkling was unearthed and edited by Dr. B. B. Kendrick, that the framers of the Fourteenth Amendment, while professing great concern for the freedmen, really conspired to sell the country "a capitalistic joker," one which achieved its purpose when in 1886 the Court recognized that the word "person" in the amendment embraced corporations.

Graham's handling of this question is scholarly and convincing. He points out, in the first place, that the author of section 1 of the Fourteenth Amendment, Representative John A. Bingham of Ohio, did not conceal, but in fact avowed, the purpose of the proposed section as not merely the protection of "American citizens of African descent," but also that of "the thousands and tens of thousands of loyal white citizens of the United States whose property, by State legislation, has been wrested from them by confiscation. . . ." In the second place, it appears that Bingham had, as early as 1856, employed the term "due process of law" in the "substantive" sense, and that he did so again in January, 1857— i.e., some weeks before the Dred Scott decision—in the course of an antislavery speech, and coupled with it the assertion that "the absolute equality of all and the equal protection of each" are the cardinal constitutional principles of American government. Finally, however, it does not appear, says Graham, that Bingham at any time applied the "due process" clause with reference to the rights of any but *natural* persons.

As to Conkling's argument, Graham shows it to have been, in its references to the purposes of the framers of the Fourteenth Amendment, an elaborate tissue of innuendoes which ingeniously avoided downright commitments, but in the course of which, nevertheless, the author of it contrived to tell what to all intents and purposes was *one* thumping lie, namely, that the "equal protection" clause had at first specified "citizens" as its beneficiaries, but that—thanks to Conkling himself—the Committee had finally substituted the word "persons." To this implication, as Graham shows, the Committee Journal lends not the slightest support. What is more, Conkling himself nowhere says explicitly that the Committee regarded corporations as "persons." Indeed, at the end he is discovered endeavoring to escape from under his own jerry-built structure of half-truths and fictions. " 'I have sought to convince your honors,' he said, 'that the men who framed . . . the Fourteenth Amendment *must have known* the meaning and force of the term "persons," and in the next sentence he spoke significantly of 'this surmise.' Later, in his peroration, he freely admitted the difficulties of the proposition he had maintained. 'The statesman,' he declared, 'has no horoscope which maps the measureless spaces of a nation's life, and lays down in advance all the bearings of its career.' Finally, he concluded in this vein, 'Those who devised the Fourteenth Amendment *may have builded better than they knew.* . . . *To some of* them, the sunset of life may have given mystical lore.' " (Italics are Graham's.)

In short, then, while the author of section 1 of the Fourteenth Amendment felt confident and in fact intended that the protection of its "due process" and "equal protection" clauses should reach *all* persons—which indeed is only its clear, literal interpretation—and while he understood better than most people did the broader significance that certain cases (some of those, e.g., which are dealt with in Chapter III *supra*) had imparted to the term "due process of law," making it a protection of the substantive as well as the procedural rights of persons, yet there is no evidence at all that he expected other than *natural* persons to receive this pro-

tection; and consequently there is no evidence that he intended to conceal such a possibility from the American public; and, equally, there is no *credible* evidence offered by
Conkling that he, another member of the Joint Committee on
Reconstruction, intended to deceive anybody at the time of
the framing of the Fourteenth Amendment, although he
certainly intended to do that very thing to the Supreme
Court when, in December, 1885, he argued the San Mateo
case (116 U.S. 138).

But was this argument of Conkling's the landmark in American constitutional history that Graham takes it to be? It
seems to me clear that it was not. The ground upon which
Graham rests his belief is the fact that in Santa Clara County
v. Southern Pacific R.R. Co. (118 U.S. 394), which was decided five months after the San Mateo case, Chief Justice
Waite announced from the Bench: "The court does not wish
to hear argument on the question whether the provision in the
Fourteenth Amendment to the Constitution, which forbids a
State to deny to any person within its jurisdiction the equal
protection of the laws, applies to these corporations. We are
all of opinion that it does."

Is this announcement, however, evidence that the Court
had been converted on this point by Conkling's argument? If
so, how are we to account for the fact that in Missouri Pacific
Ry. Co. *v.* Humes (115 U.S. 512), the Court had in November, 1885, and hence prior to Conkling's argument, consented
to take jurisdiction of a case in which a railroad corporation,
just as in the San Mateo and Santa Clara cases, was claiming
protection from State legislation which, it alleged, violated
its rights under the Fourteenth Amendment? It is true that
in the Humes case the legislation involved was sustained
while that involved in the Santa Clara case was overturned,
but this difference of outcome was clearly based on the
Court's view of the respective merits of the two cases and not
on any doubt as to its jurisdiction in the earlier case. The

fact of the matter is that the Court had taken jurisdiction of a whole series of cases in which railroad corporations had sought protection under the "due process" and "equal protection" clauses more than ten years before Conkling's argument. This was in the famous Granger cases, in seven of which the plaintiffs in error were railroad corporations; and again the decision in each instance was on the merits of the case, and not a doubt was breathed as to the Court's right to take it, either by the defendant States or by the Court. See 94 U.S. at 155, 164, 179, 180, 181.

But why should not corporations be considered "persons" in the sense of the amendment? "Corporate rights" are only a kind of shorthand for the property rights of the natural persons who own the corporations. Is it contended that people who invest in corporate securities ought to be fair prey for any marauding State legislature? It would appear, moreover, that the critics of the doctrine here being considered sometimes entirely misapprehend its practical import. It is not the doctrine of the Court that the States may not lay duties upon corporations which it may not exact of natural persons, nor yet that all corporations should be treated alike; but only that statutory discrimination between those different categories of "persons" or different types of corporations should rest on some reasonable basis. In the Santa Clara case, for example, the Court held that there was no good reason why the Southern Pacific Railroad Company should be assessed under a more burdensome rule than the rest of the railroads in the county, and in that respect the case may be taken as representative. Indeed, at times the applicability of the doctrine of "freedom of contract" to the transactions of corporations with one another has been denied. See Northern Securities Co. v. U.S., 193 U.S. 197 at 362 (1904); also Justice Peckham's opinion for the Court in Addyston Pipe and Steel Co. v. U.S., 175 U.S. 211 (1899).

I return to Campbell's argument—which, be it noted, preceded Conkling's by more than twelve years—to raise the question of the historical soundness of his contention that "laissez-faire individualism" furnished one of the mainsprings of immigration to the American Colonies. That, I suspect, is another example of what Twiss calls "lawyer's history." The impression, on the other hand, that the gospel of *laissez faire* was purely a post Civil War importation is also erroneous. The following extract from President Van Buren's Message to Congress of September 4, 1837, is certainly good laissez-faireism, even though it does not mention the term itself: "All communities are apt to look to government for too much. Even in our own country, where its powers and duties are so strictly limited, we are prone to do so, especially at periods of sudden embarrassment and distress. But this ought not to be. The framers of our excellent Constitution and the people who approved it with calm and sagacious deliberation acted at the time on a sounder principle. They wisely judged that the less government interferes with private pursuits the better for the general prosperity. It is not its legitimate object to make men rich or to repair by direct grants of money or legislation in favor of particular pursuits losses not incurred in the public service. This would be substantially to use the property of some for the benefit of others. But its real duty —that duty the performance of which makes a good government the most precious of human blessings—is to enact and enforce a system of general laws commensurate with, but not exceeding, the objects of its establishment, and to leave every citizen and every interest to reap under its benign protection the rewards of virtue, industry, and prudence." Jefferson had, in fact, said the same thing much more briefly fifty years earlier. "The policy of the American governments," he wrote, "is to leave their citizens free, neither restraining nor aiding them in their pursuits."

And Andrew Johnson's first Message to Congress, that of

December 4, 1865, which we now know to have been written
by George Bancroft, breathes the same spirit from the Jacksonian era. Dealing with the question of the relationship of the
freedmen to their recent masters, Johnson wrote: "We must
equally avoid hasty assumptions of any natural impossibility
for the two races to live side by side in a state of mutual benefit and good will. . . . The country is in need of labor, and
the freedmen are in need of employment, culture, and protection. . . . The change in their condition is the substitu-
tion of labor by contract for the status of slavery. The freed-
man can not fairly be accused of unwillingness to work so
long as a doubt remains about his freedom of choice in his
pursuits and the certainty of his recovering his stipulated
wages. In this the interests of the employer and the employed
coincide. The employer desires in his workmen spirit and
alacrity, and these can be permanently secured in no other
way. And if the one ought to be able to enforce the contract,
so ought the other. The public interest will be best promoted
if the several States will provide adequate protection and
remedies for the freedmen." And a few months later, in
his veto of the Civil Rights bill, he returned to the subject in these words: "I do not propose to consider the policy
of this bill. To me the details of the bill seem fraught
with evil. The white race and the black race of the South
have hitherto lived together under the relation of master
and slave—capital owning labor. Now, suddenly, that relation is changed, and as to ownership capital and labor are
divorced. They stand now each master of itself. In this new
relation, one being necessary to the other, there will be a new
adjustment, which both are deeply interested in making harmonious. Each has equal power in settling the terms, and if
left to the laws that regulate capital and labor it is confidently
believed that they will satisfactorily work out the problem.
Capital, it is true, has more intelligence, but labor is never so
ignorant as not to understand its own interests, not to know

its own value, and not to see that capital must pay that value."
In short, the problem of Reconstruction was to be solved by
"freedom of contract"!

The first of these passages is also interesting because it op-
poses the terms "status" and "contract" the year following
the appearance of the first American edition of Sir Henry
Maine's *Ancient Law*. On page 165 of this celebrated work
occurred the sentence: ". . . we may say that the movement of the progressive societies has hitherto been a movement from *status* to *contract*." As Dr. Twiss shows, Maine's
famous generalization furnished the text of at least two papers
before the American Bar Association during the period of the
great debate over "liberty of contract."

The notion of freedom of contract, however, appeared in
the field of constitutional interpretation long before this debate, long before the publication of *Ancient Law*, or Darwin's
Origin of Species, or Spencer's *Social Statics*. The first formulation of it that I have seen was by none other than the great
Marshall himself. In his opinion in Ogden *v.* Saunders, the
one and only time that he found himself in dissent in a constitutional case, we find him writing, in 1827: ". . . the right
to contract is the attribute of a free agent. . . . Contracts
have consequently, an intrinsic obligation. When men come
into society, they can no longer exercise this original and
natural right of coercion. It would be incompatible with
general peace, and is, therefore, surrendered. Society prohibits the use of private individual coercion, and gives in its
place a more safe and more certain remedy. But the right
to contract is not surrendered with the right to coerce performance. It is still incident to that degree of free agency
which the laws leave to every individual, and the obligation
of the contract is a necessary consequence of the right to
make it." In short, the "obligation of contracts" clause *pre-
supposes* the existence of liberty of contract (12 Wheat. 213,
350).

One further general observation:

On page 138 I remark, anent the work of the American Bar Association in indoctrinating its membership with *laissez faire*, that *"the country was presented with a new, up-to-date version of natural law."*

The question suggests itself of how this new version compares with the old, the history of which was traced in Chapter II, from its Stoic origins to Locke's elaboration of it. On first consideration, the difference between the two appears to approximate that between a *moral* code, addressed to the Reason, which it postulates as the supreme and identifying endowment of man, and "natural law" in the sense in which that term is employed by the natural sciences. The former operates *through* men; the latter *upon* men, and altogether independently of their attitude toward it, or even of their awareness of its existence. The results of its operation, as, e.g., in the case of the "law of gravitation," would therefore be of no moral significance, except for one circumstance, the assumption, to wit, that *compliance with it—whether conscious or unconscious—forwarded Progress.* Thus, according to Maine, it was *"the progressive societies"* which had heretofore moved from *status* to *contract;* while with Spencer *progressive societies* had "evolved" from the *military state* to the *industrial society*—a process not yet completed, however, or the state would have vanished. In short, the laissez-faire version of natural law contrived, in the end, to combine the *moral* prestige of the older conception with the *scientific* prestige of the newer.

INDEX